THE KOREAN WAR AND ITS LEGACY

TEACHING ABOUT KOREA THROUGH INQUIRY

THE KOREAN WAR LEGACY FOUNDATION

EDITED BY KATHY SWAN, JOHN LEE, AND S.G. GRANT

KOREAN WAR LEGACY FOUNDATION

NCSS

C3 TEACHERS
College, Career & Civic Life

FIRST PUBLISHED IN 2019.
This book is a co-publication of
National Council for the Social Studies and the Korean War Legacy Foundation.

National Council for the Social Studies
(www.socialstudies.org) is the largest professional association in the United States devoted solely to social studies education. Founded in 1921, its mission is to advocate and build capacity for high-quality social studies by providing leadership, services, and support for all social studies educators. NCSS is the publisher of the National Curriculum Standards for Social Studies and the College, Career, and Civic Life (C3) Framework for Social Studies State Standards.

The Korean War Legacy Foundation (KWLF) assists teachers, students, and the general public to understand the origins and outcomes of the Korean War, the challenges that soldiers faced while fighting it, and the legacy of the War that is exemplified by South Korea's simultaneous achievement of rapid economic development and substantive democratization in the late 20th century. KWLF offers a rich range of oral histories, documents, and historical photographs about the Korean War at https://koreanwarlegacy.org.

ISBN: 978-0-87986-115-5

Printed in the United States of America • First printing, May 2019

5   4   3   2   1

Table of
CONTENTS

PART TWO: MIDDLE-LEVEL INQUIRIES

PART THREE: HIGH SCHOOL INQUIRIES

FOREWORD

One of the main questions that I have explored in my academic career has been the need to find a convincing explanation for U.S. Secretary of State Dean Acheson's National Press Club declaration of January 12, 1950, on the American defensive perimeter in Asia that excluded Korea. A little more than five months later, on June 25, 1950, North Korea invaded the South and the Korean War began. By the end of the year, the United States was engaged in a full-scale war in Korea as the leader of a United Nations force. Many factors certainly contributed to Acheson's declaration in January, but it shaped and continues to shape the destiny of Korea.

Since my days as a young student, I have pursued two interrelated questions: What does Korea mean to the United States and what does America mean to Koreans? These are questions that may take a lifetime to answer. But part of the answer lies in the relationship that I have established with the Korean War Veterans' Association, Central New York Chapter #105 in Syracuse and with South Korea's Ministry of Patriots and Veterans Affairs (MPVA). The Korean War Veterans Digital Memorial, which is the basis for this book, is the direct outcome of my association with them, as well as with many Korean War veterans across the 50 states.

In many ways, America is responsible for the division of Korea after World War II and then for inadvertently inviting the North Korean attack in 1950. And yet it was Americans who shed blood and secured freedom for Koreans during the Korean War. Today, the Republic of Korea stands as one of the most substantial and vibrant democracies in Asia, the world's tenth largest economy, and one of the most technologically advanced countries in the world. It is impossible to imagine any of these outcomes without the sacrifices made by brave young Americans almost seventy years ago for a country that few of them knew.

On the homepage of the Korean War Veterans Digital Memorial (www.kwvdm.org), visitors will see a mosaic of the Korean Peninsula map made with photographs submitted by veterans of Central New York Chapter #105. These images challenge the statement that the Korean War is a "forgotten war" (as it is sometimes described) because, in fact, it is kept alive by the memories, experiences, and oral histories of the Korean War veterans. The photographs on the website portray many different scenes from the Korean War and Korean life, such as American soldiers fighting against Communist forces, orphaned Korean children looking through a garbage dump, and elderly Koreans in the traditional costumes of the "hermit kingdom" of nineteenth-century Korea. These images function as primary witnesses to the tragedy that exists in our memories and consciousness.

The Korean War was one of the most profound historical events of the twentieth century. Occurring early in the Cold War, the battle over Korea divided the globe into two spheres, and those divisions are still evident today. The future relationships among the combatants— South Korea, North Korea, the People's Republic of China, and the United States—are an unpainted canvas. For a positive outcome to emerge, it will take knowledge, patience, grace, and good will on the part of all.

I want to believe that a positive outcome is possible. I welcome readers to share my perspective by visiting the Korean War Veterans Digital Memorial (www.kwvdm.org) and by using the classroom inquiries in this book and the resources of the Korean War Legacy Foundation (www.koreanwarlegacy.org) to support its work and to promote the vision of peace and harmony that I believe all people are due.

Jongwoo Han

PRESIDENT, KOREAN WAR LEGACY FOUNDATION
GREEN LAKES, SYRACUSE, NY 2019

ACKNOWLEDGMENTS

As a way to preserve and commemorate the legacy of the Korean War and the honorable service of Korean War veterans, the Korean War Legacy Foundation began recording the oral histories of Korean War veterans in 2012. After starting with only 37 oral interviews, the Foundation has since accumulated about 1,400 interviews with veterans from 13 countries and has made those resources available online at https://koreanwarlegacy.org. The Foundation is now in the process of completing a collection of oral histories from all 22 Korean War participant countries by 2020 for the commemoration of the 70th anniversary of the Korean War. The project has been made possible by the Ministry of Patriots and Veterans Affairs (MPVA) of the Republic of Korea. MPVA has consistently provided not only generous funding but also strong encouragement to make this oral history collection meaningful, and has supported this Korean War Legacy Foundation publication.

This book of inquiries provides an extensive set of primary and secondary resources, as well as inquiry-based lesson plans for elementary, middle, and high school students, on the Korean War, whose legacy has been the economic development and democratization of South Korea. A distinctive feature of this book is its presentation of eyewitness accounts by Korean War veterans from the Foundation's digital archive. This curricular resource is the first of its kind created from the perspective of the soldiers, which distinguishes it from so many other publications on the Korean War. (A Google search on Korean war books produced 89,200,000 results!)

This second phase of the Foundation's work would not have been possible without the dedicated and passionate work of an expert team of social studies educators. The former President of National Council for Social Studies (NCSS), Terry Cherry, a social studies educator from Texas who was introduced to me by Dawn Blake, also from Texas, played a crucial and valuable role in introducing the Foundation to NCSS. The Foundation has worked with brilliant educators with good hearts, including Joseph Karb, who has contributed his sharp vision and extensive network to this project since we met in Rochester, midway between my home in Syracuse and his in Buffalo, during the summer of 2016.

Since then, many enthusiastic social studies teachers have explored and studied the Foundation's digital archive and have written curricular resources based on its primary sources: Barry Hayes, who leads the Foundation's fellows, Samantha Fraser, Dawn Blake, Mary Huffman, Bobbie Downs, Warren Ruiz, Maranda Wilkinson, Mariah Pol, and Valencia Robinson. The visionary scholars who were the lead writers of the C3 Framework, Professor Kathy Swan of the University of Kentucky, Professor John Lee of North Carolina State University, and Professor S.G. Grant of SUNY Binghamton, have worked with leading social studies teachers—Mona Al-Hayani, Elaine Alvey, Thomas Clouse, Carly Muetterties, and Grant Stringer—to create inquiries for this wonderful resource on the "forgotten war." NCSS Executive Director Lawrence Paska and Director of Publications Michael Simpson have been an important asset in the completion and publication of this book. I am sure that all the Korean War veterans will be very proud of this resource for our educators and future generations that records their honorable service during the Korean War.

I want to extend my sincere and deepest gratitude to the Korean War Veterans Association, its past presidents William MacSwain, Larry Kinard, Thomas Stevens, and current President Paul Cunningham and Executive Director Jim Fisher, and my many good veteran friends who fought in the Korean War. I dedicate this book to them.

Finally, I want to thank my family, who have always thought of my work as their own.

Jongwoo Han
PRESIDENT, KOREAN WAR LEGACY FOUNDATION
GREEN LAKES, SYRACUSE, NY

INTRODUCTION

Kathy Swan, John Lee, and S.G. Grant

Classroom teachers well know the challenges of bringing together the past and the present in ways that inform, challenge, and inspire their students. Those challenges can seem particularly troublesome for topics that lie outside the standard narrative of U.S. history. The Korean War is just one of those topics. With the publication of this book and the bigger project to which it is attached, however, the "forgotten war" will be forgotten no more.

"What good can come out of the Korean War?" This compelling question framed the work that resulted in this book. It is a fair question to be asked of any war experience. But it is also a complex and challenging question, for the answers can vary by time frame (immediately after, 5-10 years later, 20 years later and more), combatants (winners or losers), participants (civilians, soldiers, military leaders, policymakers, general public), and the wider world community (allies and enemies of the combatant nations). An assessment about a war's impact can also vary by disciplinary perspective—for example, a political analysis might differ radically from an economic evaluation, and an argument rooted in a single discipline might be quite different from one that draws on multiple disciplinary lenses.

The origins of this book are rooted in the Korean War Veterans Digital Memorial (KWVDM) project initiated and guided by Dr. Jongwoo Han from the Maxwell School of Citizenship and Public Affairs at Syracuse University. The KWVDM is a multi-phase effort intended to "engage the younger generation and prevent the Korean War from becoming a truly forgotten war" (http://www.kwvdm.org/about.php?p=remarks). After considerable preliminary work, the KWVDM earned secure funding in 2011 from the Ministry of Patriots and Veterans Affairs of the Republic of Korea.

At the heart of the project are U.S. Korean War veterans and their accounts of their experiences during this pivotal episode in Korean and United States history. As witnesses to history, veterans and their families provide the kinds of insights that contextualize and enliven events that can dry out on the textbook page. By interviewing the participants and archiving the recordings and associated artifacts into a searchable database, the project researchers are creating a resource for generations of historians, teachers, and students to come.

In 2012, Dr. Han created the Korean War Legacy Project (KWLP) as a way to bring the stories of Korean War veterans directly to K-12 classroom teachers and their students. The goal of the continuing project is to raise awareness of two fundamental outcomes of the Korean conflict—the emergence of South Korea as a global power and the close relationship forged between South Korea and the United States.

To advance those outcomes, the Korean War Legacy Fellowship program was created in 2017. The program brought together a dozen teacher-researchers from elementary, middle, and high schools across the United States. Directed by Mr. Joseph Karb, a nationally-recognized middle school teacher at Springville Middle School in western New York, the fellows were tasked with working through the 800 veteran interviews and 6,000 artifacts to tag and ready the materials for use in K-12 classrooms. Doing so involved the editing of interview transcripts, listing the topics covered, creating YouTube hyperlinks of selected materials, analysis of the artifacts submitted, and preparation of a short biography of each participant.

In addition to this work, a small group of fellows worked with Dr. Kathy Swan from the University of Kentucky and Dr. John Lee from North Carolina State University to create classroom inquiries for elementary, middle, and high school classrooms. An inquiry is a curriculum and teaching unit that promotes students' active engagement with powerful ideas and rich resources. Typically designed for 1-10 class periods, inquiries can be adjusted to fit any teacher's classroom conditions.

The Korean War and its Legacy brings together sets of curriculum inquiries for elementary, middle, and high school students. Drawing on an extensive range of primary and secondary sources, the inquiries take students deeply into a dozen topics that feature life in Korea, both past and present. Students delve into the history of the area, but draw equally on economic, geographic, and political insights.

Each of the curriculum inquiries is presented through a common format—the Inquiry Design Model (IDM). The IDM features a one-page blueprint on which the key questions (compelling and supporting), tasks (formative and summative), and disciplinary sources (primary and secondary) are outlined. As each chapter unfolds, the question and task elements of the blueprint are described and the sources are presented for use with students.

In Chapter 1, the Inquiry Design Model is explained through an example of one of the inquiries included in the book. Readers will understand how the questions, tasks, and sources work to support inquiry-based practice in general and how the particular questions, tasks, and sources play out across the inquiry.

Part One of the book features four inquiries designed for elementary-level classrooms. The section opens with Chapter 2 (Teaching about Korea in the Elementary Grades), which offers an overview of the elementary curriculum and describes where and how teaching about Korea can occur. The first of the inquiry chapters follows. Chapter 3 (What Is the Most Important Information a Map Can Tell Us?) employs a geographic exploration of the Korean peninsula as the vehicle for helping students consider the value of maps as representations of a range of social science data. Chapter 4 (Whose Voices Are Heard in History?) is the first of two inquiries into the nature of history. In this chapter, students investigate the role of voice in understanding history and examine how voices can gain or lose currency and how different perspectives on the past can influence our interpretations of it. Chapter 5 (What Is the Best Way to Remember History?) focuses students' attention on different elements of historical study—the several ways that history can be memorialized (or forgotten) and the ways in which historical memory can help us make better contemporary choices. And in Chapter 6 (What If You Were The Historian?), students have the opportunity to become historians as they navigate a set of oral histories and develop evidence-based claims.

In Part Two, four middle-level inquiries are featured. Chapter 7 (Teaching about Korea in the Middle Grades) sets the context for the inquiries by situating them with a typical middle school curriculum. Chapter 8 (How Does War Affect Children?) takes students into the complex topic of the experiences of children during wartime conditions and the consequences they face. In particular, they examine the role that members of the armed forces played in helping the children, and the human costs of displacement and war. In Chapter 9 (How Can Media Be Used to Influence Others?), students explore the use and misuse of media (leaflets, radio broadcasts) in the Korean War and the use and misuse of media in contemporary society, politics, and war. Chapter 10 (What Does It Mean to Sacrifice?) asks students to investigate the range of individual and group sacrifices made during times of conflict and war. Finally, Chapter 11 (Can Words Lead to War?) directs students to explore the importance words have in easing or perpetuating diplomatic tensions. More specifically, students trace the evolution of how contemporary American presidents have communicated with North Korea.

The presentation of the curriculum inquiries wraps up in Part Three. Chapter 12 (Teaching About Korea in the High School) introduces the inquiries and suggests how they might be used in the high school curriculum. The four inquiry chapters then explore a range of historical and contemporary issues. One of the outcomes of the Korean War has been the rise of huge South Korean conglomerates or *chaebols*. Chapter 13 (Are Conglomerates Good for the Economy?) focuses on the broad-brush question of whether some companies are too big to fail. Chapter 14 (Why Was the Korean War "Forgotten"?) highlights a key historical question by asking students to consider how the Korean War was different from previous and later military engagements. Chapter 15 (What Has Korea Meant to the United States?) offers students an opportunity to consider the ways in which government documents and oral histories provide unique insights into the strategic relationship between these two allies. And in Chapter 16 (How Should We Talk with North Korea?), students look at a question that U.S. presidents have negotiated from Truman to Trump.

In the Conclusion, we offer some closing thoughts about the power of teaching about Korea and the Korean War through inquiry.

CHAPTER 1

Teaching about Korea through the **Inquiry Design Model**

Kathy Swan, John Lee, and S.G. Grant

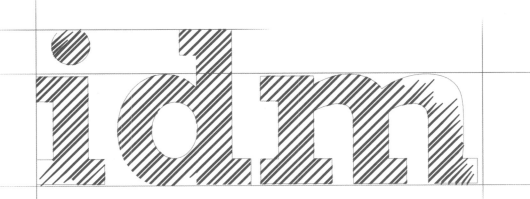

INQUIRY DESIGN MODEL

A "forgotten" war?

It's hard to imagine how a war that lasted three years, involved almost 2 million American soldiers, resulted in a higher civilian casualty rate than World War II and Vietnam, and was one of the key hot spots in the Cold War could possibly be considered "forgotten." And yet the Korean War has been characterized in that fashion since a *US News and World Report* story in October 1951 entitled "Korea: The 'Forgotten' War."

A closer look at the times both before and after the 1950-1953 "police action" provides some justification for the "forgotten" label. First, coming on the heels of a two-front war, an exhausted American populace might be excused if their attention wavered from another conflict. Second, Americans had just unconditionally defeated the mighty nations of Germany and Japan. The idea that they could they be mired in what appeared to be a civil war on the Korean peninsula seemed hard to believe. Third, heavy government censorship of the press left many Americans only vaguely aware that 37,000 American troops and between 3 and 4 million Koreans died. One other factor contributed to the forgotten nature of the war: The drawn-out and uncertain resolution to the conflict left many Americans wondering what the real outcome was. Although the U.S. (representing the UN Forces), North Korea, and China all signed onto an armistice in 1953, America's South Korean allies originally refused to do so. The active element of the war stopped but, in a technical sense, the war has yet to end.

These reasons and others help make the case for giving the Korean War slight attention. At the same time, a number of historians argue that there are even better reasons for remembering it.

First, all armed engagements have dramatic moments, but the Korean War had several. As Bruce Cumings details in his book, *The Korean War: A History*, the campaign featured bold military moves (e.g., the invasion at Inchon), and big defeats (e.g., the South Korean forces at the beginning of the war, General Douglas MacArthur's demand to bomb Chinese cities with nuclear weapons, and Harry Truman's decision to fire MacArthur within the first year of the war).[1]

A second reason to dispute the "forgotten" label is the connection between the Korean and Vietnamese wars. In her book, *In the Shadow of the Greatest Generation*, Melinda Pash argues that the shift in public perception from wide support for the war to wide disapproval first occurred around the Korean conflict. Pash shows that public opinion shifted dramatically from supporting to opposing the Korean conflict: Two-thirds of Americans supported it in late summer 1950; six months later, after the Chinese moved in, the same percentage called the war a mistake.[2]

Perhaps the strongest reason to give the Korean War its due is the fact that it set the tone and direction of relations between the U.S. and Soviet Union and between the U.S. and China for decades. The time, energy, and resources invested in the rising and falling tensions between the capitalist United States and the Communist nations of China and the Soviet Union may never be accurately calculated, but it is difficult to envision any other situation that was greater in importance in the post-World War II era. From containment to détente to cautious "frenemies" to the present, the policy shifts alone suggest that the Korean War established a set of narratives and contexts that belie the possibility of it being ignored.

One more note: The notion of the Korean War as a forgotten conflict also seems odd given its position in popular culture. Consider just two examples: The final episode of "M*A*S*H," the series featuring life in a U.S. army field hospital in the country, remains the most watched television show of all time and the Korean Veterans War Memorial is now the fourth-most visited spot in Washington DC.

And now teachers and students have one more reason to remember the Korean War—a terrific, high school-level curriculum inquiry entitled "Why Was the Korean War 'Forgotten?'" (pp. 163–185) We use that inquiry as the example in this chapter where we walk through the key components of the Inquiry Design Model (IDM). Those components—questions, tasks, and sources—provide the backbone of an inquiry and are designed to take students and their teachers deeply into the ideas, events, and actors involved in this unforgettable drama.

History, Inquiry-Based Practice, and the IDM

History as story has a rich and essential place in the transmission of human culture. And history as story continues to have a place in the teaching of social studies. Stories offer students opportunities to build knowledge, to become engaged, and to develop rich insights into why we do the things we do. The value of history as story comes with two caveats, however. One is that students need to be exposed to multiple stories, as no single narrative can communicate completely; the other is that students need to be involved in the storytelling.

Social studies classrooms have a reputation of being places where there is a single story (the textbook) told by the same storyteller (the teacher). Inquiry-based practice expands the number of stories and invites students to become the authors of their own narratives. Those narratives take any number of forms but, at heart, each advances an evidence-based story or argument.

To help teachers and students work their way into these possibilities, the Inquiry Design Model highlights the three elements typically found in inquiry-based classrooms—genuine questions, rich sources, and meaningful tasks. There is more to the IDM than this simple list, but without attending to each of these components, teachers' and students' inquiry-based efforts are likely to flounder.

There are other reasons as well. Inquiry-based practice demands a fair amount of planning time. Teachers worry that students may not succeed on more challenging assignments. Standardized testing seems to reward traditional teaching approaches. These challenges are not insignificant. The research literature, however, strongly supports inquiry-based practice as a powerful approach to teaching and learning.[3] Moreover, the benefits of engaging in inquiry accrue to all students—elementary, secondary, and academically challenged as well as academically gifted.[4]

Empirical findings are important, but they will convince few teachers to take the inquiry plunge unless doing so can fit into their everyday practices. If teachers are going to engage in inquiry-based practice, then they need to have clear and helpful models.

The Inquiry Design Model (IDM) attends to each of these challenges. As a concise, practical approach to developing classroom inquiries, IDM offers teachers a means of seeing their way into inquiry-based practice.[5] And with a bank of over 200 inquiries available at C3Teachers.org to draw on, teachers can save considerable planning time.

The Inquiry Design Model is rooted in the blueprint, a one-page representation of the common elements of inquiry-based practice—questions, tasks, and sources. The blueprint offers a visual snapshot of an entire inquiry such that the individual components and the relationship among the components can all be seen at once. As such, they focus on the following elements necessary to support students as they address a compelling question using disciplinary sources in a thoughtful and informed fashion:

- Standards (anchor the content of the inquiry);

- Compelling questions (frame the inquiry);

- Staging the compelling question tasks (create interest in the inquiry)

- Supporting questions (develop the key content);

- Formative performance tasks (demonstrate emerging understandings);

- Featured sources (provide opportunities to generate curiosity, build knowledge, and construct arguments);

- Summative performance tasks (demonstrate evidence-based arguments);

- Summative extensions (offer assessment flexibility);

- Taking informed action exercises (promote opportunities for civic engagement).

In the sections that follow, we unpack the defining elements of inquiry—questions, tasks and sources—relevant to an inquiry on how historical events are deemed worthy of remembering in general and why the Korean War has been "forgotten" in particular. In doing so, we highlight the compelling and supporting questions that frame and organize this inquiry; the formative and summative assessment tasks that provide opportunities for students to demonstrate and apply their understandings; and the disciplinary sources that allow students to practice disciplinary thinking and reasoning (See Figure 1).

Figure 1: IDM Blueprint

Structured Inquiry

	COMPELLING QUESTION
C3 Framework Indicator	
Staging the Compelling Question	

Supporting Question 1	Supporting Question 2	Supporting Question 3
Formative Performance Task	Formative Performance Task	Formative Performance Task
Featured Sources	Featured Sources	Featured Sources

Summative Performance Task	ARGUMENT
	EXTENSION
Taking Informed Action	UNDERSTAND
	ASSESS
	ACT

The Power of Questions

Ideas are at the heart of all good instruction; ideas expressed in the form of questions provide the framing for inquiry-based instruction. Questions come in two forms in the Inquiry Design Model (IDM)—compelling and supporting. Different in form and function, these two kinds of questions nevertheless work together to build academic rigor and student relevance into an inquiry.

Rigor and relevance—good compelling questions have to hit both of those marks. Rigorous questions reflect an enduring issue, concern, or debate in history—an idea worth spending some time with and some intellectual energy on. For example, the compelling question "Why Was the Korean War 'Forgotten?'" uses the Korean conflict as a vehicle for exploring the issue of what it means to remember historical events and, more generally, the socially constructed nature of history. Far from a simple chronology of one event after another, history is an interpretive discipline, one in which historians weigh evidence from multiple sources, draw conclusions, and make evidence-based arguments. If students are to understand historical events, then they need to understand the nature of history as a field of inquiry.

Making sense of often conflicting information is key to the work that historians do; it also defines much of what high school students do on a daily basis as they navigate their lives inside and outside of school. A question about the forgotten status of an event that was presumably important asks students to sort through a range of data, perspectives, and ideas—in this case, in service of determining whether the Korean War was or was not worth being remembered. Connecting the academic with the social, a compelling question offers insights into both the larger world and the immediate context in which students live.

Compelling questions establish the overall framework for an inquiry; supporting questions define the content that fills out that frame. Representing a logical flow of ideas, supporting questions enable students to generate content-based understandings. Students then employ those understandings in the construction of their evidence-based arguments.

In the inquiry "Why Was the Korean War 'Forgotten?,'" (pp. 163–185) the sequence of supporting questions demonstrates a contrasting perspectives logic where students have an opportunity to see how differing views—the general public, the soldiers who fought, and the authors of U.S. history textbooks—compare and contrast:

1. How did the Korean conflict become a "war"?

2. What domestic concerns distracted Americans from the war?

3. Did the soldiers forget?

4. How has U.S. history forgotten the Korean War?

After establishing the relevant events in Supporting Question 1, teachers and their students begin looking at the Korean War from different angles. Supporting Question 2 directs students to explore the range of domestic issues during the early 1950s that could have pulled attention away from the Korean situation. The perspective on Korea shifts to that of soldiers on the ground in Supporting Question 3. One last perspective—that of textbook authors—offers students yet one more vantage point on the question of why the Korean War appears to have been forgotten.

As is the case in most inquiries, this set of compelling and supporting questions are mutually interacting—the compelling question frames the inquiry and the supporting questions give it a coherent internal structure. Of course, there are any number of possible compelling questions on the Korean War and an equal number of supporting question sequences. We invite teachers to consider this example of compelling and supporting questions, but to tweak them as befits their classroom situations.

The Role of Tasks

If compelling and supporting questions set the stage for learning, formative and summative tasks enable students to demonstrate their learning. Because the IDM tasks serve instructional as well as evaluative purposes, the range of performance tasks, extension activities, and opportunities for taking informed action offer teachers multiple opportunities to see how their students are making sense of the inquiry's compelling and supporting questions.

An IDM inquiry begins with a compelling question and ends with students making an argument. As a result, students' summative products are convergent—that is, the work they do in the inquiry converges on the construction of evidence-based arguments that address the compelling question. The formative performance tasks students undertake in response to each supporting question can also be considered convergent in nature, as this work helps students develop and support their arguments

Convergent thinking is necessary, but not sufficient. An IDM inquiry also includes opportunities for divergent thinking through the extension activities and taking informed action exercises. In these tasks, students are offered opportunities to expand the presentation of their ideas.

Central to the process of crafting an evidence-based argument are content and skills students develop throughout an inquiry. Toward that end, formative performance tasks function as content and skill exercises intended to scaffold students toward the goal of making and supporting their arguments. Tasks do not include all of what students might need to know and do, but they do include the major content and skills that are necessary to producing their arguments.

The formative performance tasks in the inquiry "Why Was the Korean War 'Forgotten?'" follow directly from the supporting questions. In doing so, they provide opportunities for students to develop the knowledge (e.g., understanding the many perspectives on the Korean War) and practice the skills (e.g., reading sources and supporting claims with evidence). Following the logic of contrasting perspectives in response to the supporting questions, the formative performance tasks ask students to:

1. Create an annotated timeline of the major events that led to the Korean War.

2. Write a paragraph that describes the domestic concerns that distracted Americans from the Korean conflict.

3. Write a claim supported by evidence about why soldiers believe the war was "forgotten."

4. Write an evidence-based claim or series of claims as to how the Korean War has or has not been forgotten in U.S. history.

More than a set of arbitrary end-of-chapter questions, formative performance tasks enable students to build the content knowledge and skills relevant to the work that underlies their summative arguments.

In addition to the convergent work behind the formative performance tasks are divergent tasks such as the summative extension. Although it reflects the overall purpose of the inquiry in general and the students' arguments in particular, an extension activity offers students a chance to flex their creative muscles. Extensions can take any number of forms— graphic, textual, oral, and even performances. Important to keep in mind, however, is the idea that the extension offers students a chance to reuse their initial arguments in a new form. In the inquiry "Why Was the Korean War 'Forgotten?,'" the extension activity asks students to use the claims that they developed in response to Supporting Question 4 to propose a revision to a textbook that adds the perspectives of U.S. soldiers.

The last type of IDM task is taking informed action. Offered as an opportunity to engage the content of an inquiry in an active civic form, these exercises work in a variety of contexts both inside and outside of the classroom. Central to any action activity, however, is the idea that it is *informed:* Students build their knowledge and understanding of the issue behind the compelling question before engaging in any type of social action. In the *understand* stage, students demonstrate that they can think about the issues behind the inquiry in a new setting or context. The *assess* stage asks students to consider alternative perspectives, scenarios, or options as they begin to define a possible set of actions. And the *act* stage is where students decide if and how they will put into effect the results of their planning. For the inquiry "Why Was the Korean War 'Forgotten?,'" the sequence for taking informed action is:

UNDERSTAND: Explore the Interview Initiative of the *Korean War Veterans Digital Memorial Project (KWVDMP)* and identify local veteran groups or other community members who are Korean War veterans.

ASSESS: Determine the ways in which students can contribute to the initiative.

ACT: Create an oral history project to contribute to the KWVDM archives.

The three taking informed action stages put students in the position to transfer their understandings from the inquiry directly to a contemporary issue and to make decisions about how they might use their voices to participate in public discourse around the matter.

The Significance of Sources

Questions and tasks define two of the three key components of an inquiry. As the third, sources provide students with access to the substance and content behind the inquiry topic. With a set of disciplinary sources in hand, students can dig into the ideas and apply their analytical skills to move the inquiry forward.

Sources play three roles in an inquiry: 1) to spark and sustain student curiosity in an inquiry; 2) to build students' disciplinary (content and conceptual) knowledge and skills; and 3) to enable students to construct arguments with evidence. Used in this fashion, sources support each part of the IDM blueprint: staging the compelling question, formative performance tasks, summative performance tasks, and additional summative tasks (i.e., extensions and taking informed action exercises).

One way sources can be used to spark students' curiosity is through the staging activity. In the inquiry "Why Was the Korean War 'Forgotten?,'" for example, students are given an excerpted version of the 1951 *US News and World Report* article that introduced the idea of the Korean conflict as a "forgotten" war and four examples of monuments that employ the word. Based on these sources, students can brainstorm ideas about the political, social, and cultural factors that influence decisions about, if, and how historical events are remembered. The images also introduce students to the notion that different groups may have different ideas about the act of remembering.

A second use for sources is in helping students build their disciplinary knowledge and skills. Although content and conceptual knowledge are important, students also need to learn and practice disciplinary skills such as historical thinking and geographic reasoning if they are to fully realize the goals of inquiry. Debating which is more important, content or skills, is pointless; students need both. They have opportunities to gain both through the use of sources to complete formative and summative tasks.

Students encounter a range of disciplinary sources within the inquiry "Why Was the Korean War 'Forgotten?'" They work with a range of primary sources (e.g., photographs of Korean War memorials, oral histories, a radio speech) and secondary accounts (e.g., magazine and newspaper articles, histories, textbook entries). Working with and through this range of sources, students complete formative tasks and accumulate the ideas and evidence necessary to make and support their claims and arguments. In doing so, they realize the third use of disciplinary sources.

The wealth and availability of sources holds considerable promise for inquiry-based teaching and learning. Yet, sources typically were not created with a classroom inquiry in mind or with high school students as the intended audience. As a result, more often than not, some kind of adaptation of sources needs to occur to meet students' needs. True, some sources—artwork, videos, and photographs, for example—may not need any treatment. Many others, however, may require adaptation in order to meet students' disparate academic needs. Some of those needs can be attended to by scaffolds (e.g., SCIM-C).[6] Others can be supported by adapting the sources in any of three ways:

- *Excerpting*—involves using a portion of the source for the inquiry. Care should be taken to preserve information in the source that students may need to know about the creator and context of the source.

- *Modifying*—involves inserting definitions and/or changing the language of a text. Modifying texts increases students' accessibility to sources.

- *Annotating*—involves adding short descriptions or explanations in order to introduce a text or to explain a challenging concept. Annotations allow teachers to set a background context for sources.

In the inquiry "Why Was the Korean War 'Forgotten?'" several of the text sources and oral histories have been excerpted in ways that highlight the key elements students will need to complete the formative performance tasks. If interested, teachers can make the full texts available so that interested students can pursue their understandings.

Some observers object to altering sources on the grounds that doing so invariably alters meaning. It is a valid concern. At the same time, teachers should keep in mind the purpose of the source in the inquiry and ask themselves whether they are using the source for the source's sake or to accomplish their learning goal. It will be the rare occasion when a teacher uses a source solely for the sake of employing it in its original form.

Bringing It All Together

Inquiry-based practice, with its requisite attention to questions, tasks, and sources asks much of teachers and their students. The research evidence, however, consistently demonstrates that students of all ages and of all ability groups can profit from opportunities to engage in inquiry.[7] There is no single way to build an inquiry-based teaching practice, but with the Inquiry Design Model, teachers can see how questions, tasks, and sources work individually and together to create opportunities for all their students to succeed.

The guidance within each IDM-designed inquiry is considerable, but it is not exhaustive. Research and our own experience tell us that teachers teach best the material that they mold around their particular students' needs and the contexts in which they teach. Good teachers need no scripts. The IDM, therefore, encourages teachers to draw on the wealth of their teaching knowledge and experience to add to and modify activities, lessons, sources, and tasks that transform the inquiries into their own, individual pedagogical plans.

The inquiries in this book come in two forms. "Why Was the Korean War 'Forgotten?'" is an example of a *structured* inquiry. In the original version of the Inquiry Design Model, a structured inquiry is built out with the questions, tasks, and sources intended for 5-10 days of instruction. A *focused* inquiry, by contrast, is designed for a shorter period of time, typically 1-2 days.[8] Focused inquiries are a means by which teachers can help their students build their inquiry skills even if they are pressed for time.

Conclusion

In this chapter, we use the components of the Inquiry Design Model to illustrate the possibilities of inquiry-based practice in general and a more ambitious approach to teaching about the Korean War in particular. This inquiry and the others featured in this book have been developed with the challenges that practicing teachers face firmly in mind. But also in the center of our minds are stories of teachers who have described, sometimes with tears in their eyes, how their inquiry-based attempts brought even their most reluctant students into rich and powerful discussions. Inquiry brings together teachers, students, and ideas, and, taken together, this combination can be electric.

NOTES

1. B. Cumings, *The Korean War: A History* (New York: Modern Library, 2011).

2. M. Pash, *In the Shadow of the Greatest Generation: The Americans Who Fought the Korean War* (New York: NYU Press, 2014).

3. S.G. Grant, K. Swan, and J. Lee, *Inquiry-based Practice in Social Studies Education: The Inquiry Design Model* (New York: Routledge, 2017).

4. S.G. Grant, "Teaching Practices in History Education," in S. Metzger & L. Harris (Eds.), *International Handbook of History Teaching and Learning* (New York: Wiley-Blackwell, 2018), 419-448.

5. K. Swan, J. Lee, and S.G. Grant, *Inquiry Design Model: Building Inquiries in Social Studies* (Silver Spring, MD: National Council for the Social Studies and C3 Teachers, 2018).

6. The SCIM-C Strategy focuses on Summarizing, Contextualizing, Inferring, Monitoring, and Corroborating. See David Hicks, Peter E. Doolittle, and E. Thomas Ewing, "The SCIM-C Strategy: Expert Historians, Historical Inquiry, and Multimedia," *Social Education* 68, no. 3 (April 2004), 221-226.

7. S.G. Grant, "Teaching Practices in History Education," 419-448.

8. K. Swan, J. Lee, and S.G. Grant, "Questions, Tasks, Sources: Focusing on the Essence of Inquiry," *Social Education* 82, no. 3 (May-June 2018), 142-146.

PART ONE

ELEMENTARY-LEVEL INQUIRIES

CHAPTER 2

Teaching about Korea in the **Elementary Grades**

Kathy Swan, John Lee, and S.G. Grant

If Korea and the Korean War have typically gained little attention in the secondary school curriculum, few observers will be surprised to learn that the typical elementary program of studies offers few obvious prospects for younger students to explore these topics. The reasons for this omission are varied and complex,[1] and the idea that Korea will ever play a major role in the curriculum is unlikely. The good news, however, is that there are opportunities for teachers to use the content of Korean culture in general and the Korean War in particular to create engaging instructional possibilities for elementary-aged students.

Despite long-standing and sometimes scathing criticism,[2] the elementary school curriculum in the United States has endured. Since the 1930s, the dominant curriculum model for teaching young children has been Paul Hanna's "expanding communities" approach. This model is based on the notion that children's awareness and interest work steadily outward from themselves to their family and communities, and then on to the state and nation. Advocates claim that this spiraling approach moves students from their most familiar environs to increasingly more complex contexts.[3] Some critics, however, assert that the model is non-informative and superficial.[4] Others argue that the curriculum sends signals that young students are not ready to grapple with more rigorous and debatable content so teachers should focus on "safe topics."[5] Over the past couple of decades, researchers have challenged this traditional mindset by documenting young students' capacity to engage in authentic historical inquiry and critical thinking.[6] Change comes slowly to schools, however, so the expanding communities model remains the "de facto national curriculum."[7]

On the surface, the elementary school curriculum offers no clear spot to introduce the study of Korea. Still, there are opportunities to do so. One of those opportunities is at the third grade level. The typical third-grade curriculum is organized around the theme of communities around the world. The idea is that teachers build on their students' K-2 knowledge and experiences of learning about families, neighborhoods, and their local communities. Expanding the notion of a community to the wider world stage creates opportunities for teachers to use Korea as one of the case studies of a non-United States-based culture. In addition to Korean food and festivals, students and their teachers could explore aspects of language, music, clothing, customs, and traditions and their intersectionality in our global world. For example, popular K-Pop music finds its roots in styles and genres from around the world, including jazz, gospel, hip-hop, reggae, folk, country, and classical as well as traditional Korean music. Also unique to Korea is the "hanbok," a traditional style dress worn for formal occasions including a child's first birthday, a wedding, or a funeral. As fashion trends come and go in both the U.S. and Korea, the hanbok remains a ceremonial garment in Korea today. Exploring these unique cultural aspects of Korean society allows students to make direct comparisons with similar dimensions of other cultures.

A more explicit connection to the third-grade curriculum can be made to the inquiry in Chapter 3 of this collection. That inquiry features the compelling question "What Is the Most Important Information a Map Can Tell Us?" Geographic concepts are well within the reach of even very young children who can develop mental maps of their immediate surroundings and use simple mapping systems.[8] Still, some misconceptions that students have about place and space can persist without their teachers' skilled guidance:

Simply telling children to change their intuitive, but counter-productive spatial ideas does little good. They need opportunities in the presence of knowledgeable others to engage in spatial-reasoning investigations (e.g., drawing and describing their own mental maps and making map representations based on data collected or personal field observations) in which they confront cognitive impasses created by their naïve everyday ideas.[9]

The inquiry around mapping in this book gives students an opportunity to refresh their knowledge of map symbols and legends, but it then moves on to the use of maps to examine key elements of Korean society. Using a series of maps, students learn about the political, economic, and historical elements of Korea, as well as key geographic landforms. The inquiry concludes with students making an argument in response to the compelling question. Doing so offers them an occasion to employ their new knowledge in ways that speak to a more engaging purpose than simply recalling the information on a multiple-choice exam.

The three other inquiries in this section aim at a higher elementary grade level. Fifth grade is typically the first year of sustained study of history and United States history is typically the content focus. Content is important, but so are the skills and dispositions that students develop through disciplinary study. Students explore the nature of history through two inquiries in this section: Chapter 4 (Whose Voices Are Heard in History?) and Chapter 5 (What Is the Best Way to Remember History?). The final chapter in this section (What If You Were The Historian?) offers students the opportunity to demonstrate their new knowledge and skills as they examine a set of oral histories and develop evidence-based claims.

Helping students learn how to develop and support arguments is a central instructional focus of history education.[10] But other elements of history are also important to explore. One of those elements is the notion of perspective. Among the reasons that students have long rated social studies as one of their least favorite school subjects[11] is that it typically presents history as a straight-line narrative told from the perspective of a single, omnipresent observer.[12] Children know from their lived experiences that every story can be authored in different ways, so learning that an historical event might be viewed differently from different vantage points will not surprise them. That said, students will need their teacher's steady instructional hand to appreciate and understand the full value of exploring the multiple perspectives.

Here, we briefly describe the elementary-level inquiries that are presented later in this section of the book.

To that end, the inquiry in Chapter 4 explores the compelling question "Whose Voices Are Heard in History?" The question is framed broadly; the inquiry takes students directly into a case study using the Korean War. Here, students learn that the "forgotten war" also includes a number of groups whose experiences are often forgotten. African-American soldiers and women in the armed services and at home also have perspectives that demand consideration when understanding the wartime situation in Korea. Answering the compelling question behind this inquiry gives students a chance to make arguments about the value of perspective.

In Chapter 5, students look at the nature of history from a different angle—how an historical event is memorialized. As with the notion of perspective, young students may struggle a bit to understand that history is represented in a variety of ways. History texts are one, but they are hardly the only one.[13] The compelling question for the chapter—"What Is the Best Way to Remember History?"—exposes students to several venues—monuments, songs, and oral histories—that students might now realize offer useful insights into the unfolding of the Korean War. As they construct their arguments in response to the compelling questions, students may conclude that there is no one "best" way to appreciate the war. But in developing their responses, they wrestle with the key challenge of how to represent the past.

The final inquiry in this first section highlights the active role that historians play in understanding and relating historical events. The compelling question behind the chapter—"What If You Were The Historian?"—gives students an opportunity to practice a key historian's skill—corroboration of sources. Although this inquiry might be conducted independently from those profiled in Chapters 4 and 5, in several ways, it forms a lovely extension of the knowledge and skills that students develop through those earlier inquiries. In brief, the "Historian" inquiry asks students to make judgments about the voices and perspectives evident on a Korean War topic and to consider how those voices and perspectives reinforce or repudiate one another. Such reasoning may be deemed too sophisticated for fifth-graders, but researchers demonstrate that teachers often underestimate students' abilities.[14]

Before presenting the inquiries, let us take a moment to point out some of their principal features. Highlighting these should help readers take better advantage of the full instructional value that the inquiries represent.

First, as noted in Chapter 1, the elementary-focused inquiries give equal attention to both academic rigor and student relevance. In the descriptions above, we spent more time on the former than the latter. That said, the compelling questions in each of the four inquiries speak to one or more ways to provoke students' interest. For example, the "Most Important Information" and "Best Way to Remember" inquiries play on the idea of challenging students to argue for a single preeminent idea. That they may decide, in both cases, that there is no one best or most important conclusion does not undercut the enthusiasm that students typically bring to such assignments. The "Voices" and "Historian" inquiries also draw on similar ways to engage students' attention. Because they are acutely aware that adults often dismiss them as mere children, students know what it is like to have their perspectives ignored. To ratify the points that there is always more than one vantage point on an event and that hearing more perspectives helps us better understand those events will likely strike students as significant.

A second feature of the elementary inquiries is that they focus as much on building students' skills as they do on building their content knowledge. For too long, educators have debated the prominence of content versus skills. That debate cannot be sustained: Both are important. In short, we learn content through the skills we employ and we learn skills by practicing them on content. The content in these four inquiries is clear—the geographic, economic, and political past and present in Korea. Equally clear are the opportunities to strengthen students' geographic and historical skills in combination with their reading and writing skills. Students will not master any of these skills as elementary students, but the foundations they build should prove invaluable in later years.

The extensive use of the oral histories of Korean War veterans and their families is a third feature of the elementary inquiries. Although the middle and high school inquiries also take advantage of this rich resource, introducing what is likely to be an unknown kind of source to elementary-aged students is novel. Young students know how to glean information from visual and written texts, but their worlds are still largely oral in nature. To have access to the traces of history through the Korean War Legacy Project archives is likely to surprise and delight them.

One last feature of the elementary inquiries worth noting is the option in Chapter 6 for students to engage in some self-directed study. Teachers can have their students pursue the topic described in the inquiry (racism among the U.S. troops), but they may also choose to allow their students to explore topics of their own choice. Choice matters to children, which is one reason why they typically respond so positively to the idea of making supporting arguments—that is, their own arguments. So to offer them the opportunity to define what they learn signals the power that choice holds.

The study of Korea may not be a staple in elementary school classrooms, but it can be. These four inquiries offer students opportunities to explore both contemporary and historical components of Korean society. They also offer students opportunities to continue developing their content and literary skills in ways that honor and support each. Ultimately, these curriculum experiences allow students to inquire and this may be their greatest contribution—to wrestle with a question about the world and the people that live in it.

NOTES

1. L. LeRiche, "The Expanding Environments Sequence in Elementary Social Studies: The Origins," *Theory and Research in Social Education* 15, no. 3(1987), 137-154.

2. D. Ravitch, "Tot Sociology: Or What Happened to History in the Grade Schools," *American Scholar* 56, no. 3 (1987), 343-354.

3. J. Stallones, "Paul Hanna and Expanding Communities," *International Journal of Social Education* 18, no. 2 (2003-2004), 33-43.

4. B. Bisland, "Two Traditions in the Social Studies Curriculum for the Elementary Grades: The Textbooks of Paul Hanna and Harold O. Rugg," *Journal of Social Studies Research* 33, no. 2 (2009), 155-196; J. Brophy and J. Alleman, "A Reconceptualized Rationale for Elementary Social Studies," *Theory and Research in Social Education* 34, no. 4 (2006), 428-454; R. Wade, "Beyond Expanding Horizons: New Curriculum Directions for Elementary Social Studies," *Elementary School Journal* 103, no. 2(2002), 115-130.

5. M. P. Ghiso, "Arguing from Experience: Young Children's Embodied Knowledge and Writing as Inquiry," *Journal of Literacy Research* 47, no. 2 (2015), 186–215.

6. Ghiso, "Arguing from Experience: Young Children's Embodied Knowledge and Writing as Inquiry"; L. S. Levstik and K. C. Barton, *Doing History: Investigating with Children in Elementary and Middle Schools* (New York: Routledge, 2011); B. VanSledright, *In Search of America's Past: Learning to Read History in Elementary School* (New York: Teachers College Press, 2002).

7. J. Brophy, "Teaching Social Studies for Understanding and Higher Order Applications," *The Elementary School Journal* 90, no. 4 (1990), 351-417.

8.   S. Bednarz, G. Acheson, and R. Bednarz, "Maps and Map Learning in Social Studies," in W. Parker (Ed.), *Social Studies Today: Research and Practice* (New York: Routledge, 2010), 121-132.

9.   National Council for the Social Studies (NCSS), *The College, Career, and Civic Life (C3) Framework for Social Studies State Standards* (Silver Spring, MD: NCSS, 2013), 86.

10.   National Council for the Social Studies (NCSS), *The College, Career, and Civic Life (C3) Framework for Social Studies State Standards*, op.cit.

11.   M. Schug, R. Todd, and R. Beery, "Why Kids Don't Like Social Studies," *Social Education* 47, no. 5 (1984), 382-387.

12.   R. J. Paxton, "A Deafening Silence: History Textbooks and the Students Who Read Them," *Review of Educational Research* 69, no. 3 (1999), 315-339.

13.   National Council for the Social Studies (NCSS), *The College, Career, and Civic Life (C3) Framework for Social Studies State Standards*, op. cit.

14.   R. Ferretti, C. MacArthur, and C. M. Okolo, "Teaching for Historical Understanding in Inclusive Classrooms," *Learning Disabilities Quarterly* 24 (2001), 59-71; B. VanSledright, *The Challenge of Rethinking History Education: On Practices, Theories, and Policy* (New York: Routledge, 2011).

What Is the **Most Important Information** a Map Can Tell Us?

Elaine Alvey and Kathy Swan

WHAT IS THE MOST IMPORTANT INFORMATION A MAP CAN TELL US?

C3 Framework Indicator	**D2. Geo.3.K-2**. Use maps, globes, and other simple geographic models to identify cultural and environmental characteristics of places.
Staging the Compelling Question	Teachers will show students a National Geographic video clip on how maps are made, and have students find their location and the location of South Korea and/or the Korean Peninsula on a map.

SUPPORTING QUESTION 1	SUPPORTING QUESTION 2
What are the common characteristics of a map?	What can we learn about Korea by studying maps?
FORMATIVE PERFORMANCE TASK	**FORMATIVE PERFORMANCE TASK**
Create a list of the common characteristics of a map (e.g., title, scale, symbols, cities, rivers).	Share observations about the map set with a partner and write down two of these observations.
FEATURED SOURCES	**FEATURED SOURCES**
Source A: Political map of North America **Source B:** "South Up" world map **Source C:** Map of the Korean Peninsula **Source D:** Population density map of South Korea	**Source A:** Gapminder mapping tool **Source B:** Political map of Southeast Asia **Source C:** Historical map of Korean Peninsula (1730 C.E.) **Source D:** Map of major Korean rivers

Summative Performance Task	**ARGUMENT** What is the most important thing that maps can teach us about Korea? Construct an argument in the form of a poster or drawing that addresses the compelling question.
	EXTENSION Construct an argument about the most important information maps can tell us about the world, or generalizing the case study of Korea to the broader use of maps.
Taking Informed Action	**UNDERSTAND** Discuss the idea that maps can be an important part of telling a story about a community.
	ASSESS Compare a variety of local/community maps drawn at different scales or focusing on different features, and determine the advantages of some maps over others.
	ACT Create a map of your community including the most important information you would want someone to know about places in the community.

Overview
Inquiry Description

This inquiry leads students through an investigation of maps, the common characteristics of maps, and the stories maps can tell about a place. By investigating the compelling question, "What is the most important information a map can tell us?," students evaluate a set of maps with a focus on the Korean Peninsula as a case study. The formative performance tasks build on knowledge and skills through the course of the inquiry, help students deepen their understanding of maps and their value as a tool for understanding the world, and build content knowledge about the Korean Peninsula. Using the map set provided, students create an evidence-based argument about the most important piece of information they learned.

This inquiry is designed to provide students with an introduction to maps as a resource and to the Korean Peninsula. This focused inquiry should not require prerequisite knowledge; however some of the maps involve concepts that students may need some scaffolding to understand.

This inquiry is expected to take one to two 30-minute class periods. The inquiry time frame could expand if teachers think their students need additional instructional experiences (i.e., supporting questions, formative performance tasks, and featured sources). Teachers may want to include other classroom resources in the exploration of maps; these might include globes, community maps, or other locally relevant tools and resources. Teachers are encouraged to adapt the inquiries in order to meet the requirements and interests of their particular students. Resources can also be modified as necessary to meet individualized education programs (IEPs) or Section 504 plans for students with disabilities.

Structure of the Inquiry

In addressing the compelling question, "What is the most important information a map can tell us?," students work through a series of supporting questions, formative performance tasks, and featured sources in order to construct an argument supported by evidence.

STAGING THE COMPELLING QUESTION

In staging the compelling question, teachers may provide students with one or both of the resources provided. The first featured source is a video clip from National Geographic about historical mapmaking processes. Teachers may want to use this video to highlight some of the most important concepts around the common features of most maps (e.g., key, title, scale, compass rose). The second featured source is a map highlighting North America and East Asia. Because this compelling question includes a case study of Korea, this map has been provided so students can find their location (state, community, or region) and then find Korea. This helps students begin to see the relative locations of these places, which provides a grounding for the rest of the sources and supporting questions.

SUPPORTING QUESTION 1

In answering the first supporting question, "What are the common characteristics of maps?," students analyze a set of maps and identify the common characteristics they find. These characteristics might include title, compass rose, or other features. The formative performance task asks students to create a list of these characteristics. The featured sources for this question provide a variety of world and regional maps that include a range of information, but support students in identifying common map features. The featured documents include a political map of North America, a "South up" world map, a detailed map of the Korean Peninsula, and a population-density map. The political map of North America and the population-density map include compasses, titles, keys and scales. These maps also work to further students' understanding of the Korean Peninsula so that they can grapple with the case study of this country and develop their answers to the central compelling question of this inquiry.

SUPPORTING QUESTION 2

The second supporting question is, "What can we learn about Korea by studying maps?" Students discuss this question with a team and then make a bulleted list of the facts they observe about Korea from the set of maps. In addition to the resources from the previous supporting question, the featured sources provide students with additional materials that allow them to build an understanding of Korea. It may be appropriate to have students use other classroom resources, such as a globe, atlas, or wall map. Each of these featured sources helps build students' understanding of Korea so that they can evaluate the compelling question using Korea as a case study. The featured sources include a global map created with the Gapminder mapping tool, a Southeast Asia political map, a historical map (1730 C.E.), and a map of the major rivers of the Korean Peninsula.

SUMMATIVE PERFORMANCE TASK

At this point in the inquiry, students have examined a variety of maps: global and regional, as well as political, physical, and thematic.

Students should be expected to demonstrate the breadth of their understanding and their ability to use evidence from multiple sources to support their claims. In this task, students construct an evidence-based argument using multiple sources to answer the compelling question, "What is the most important information maps can tell us?" It is important to note that students' arguments could take a variety of forms, including a drawing or oral presentation, particularly for young students who struggle with writing.

Students' arguments will likely vary, but could include any of the following:

- The most important thing we can learn from a map is the location of places around the world.

- The most important information is related to the economy or industry of a country.

- The most important thing we can learn is information about the physical geography (rivers, oceans, mountains).

- We can learn about cities and populations by studying maps.

- We can learn something about what life is like for people around the world (language, climate, income, industry) by studying maps.

- We can learn about the history of a community or country by studying maps.

To extend their arguments, teachers may have students construct an argument about the most important information maps can tell us about the world, or generalize from their case study of Korea to the broader use of maps.

Students have the opportunity to take informed action by drawing on their understandings that maps can provide important and interesting information about a place. To understand, students can engage in a teacher-led discussion on the idea that maps can be an important part of telling a community's story. To assess maps as storytelling tools and resources to communicate key data, students can assess maps of their local communities and consider what story is being told, what data are available, and how maps contribute to our understanding. To act, students can create a map of their own community that includes the most important information they want to share about their community.

For further reading on community mapmaking with elementary learners, a good reference is David Sobel's *Mapmaking with Children: Sense of Place Education for the Elementary Years* (Portsmouth, NH: Heinemann, 1998).

Children's literature that includes themes of community mapmaking might also be helpful to young students as they engage with this question. Examples include:

- DyAnne DiSalvo-Ryan. *Grandfather's Corner Store*. New York: HarperCollins, 2000.

- Joan Sweeney. *Me on the Map*. New York: Knopf Books for Young Readers, 2014.

- Loreen Leedy. *Mapping Penny's World*. New York: Henry Holt and Company, 2000.

Staging the Compelling Question

FEATURED SOURCE Source A: National Geographic video.

https://news.nationalgeographic.com/2018/01/road-map-vintage-video-1940-mapmakers-cartography/

Making road maps might seem like a mundane or even obsolete task today, but this 1940 video on the National Geographic website portrays it as a heroic endeavor. The gung-ho narrator describes how draftsmen continuously updated maps based on reports from "road scouts" who drove the country's fast-expanding road network and sent back details on route changes: "It's swell teamwork on the part of everyone that gets speedy, accurate information on modern road maps!"

After viewing the video, students should use classroom resources, maps, globes or Google Maps like the map of North America and Asia featured on this page to find their location (state, community, or region) and then find Korea. This serves as an introduction for students to see the relative locations of these places to provide a grounding for remaining sources and supporting questions.

Staging the Compelling Question

FEATURED SOURCE Source B: Google map of North America and Asia.

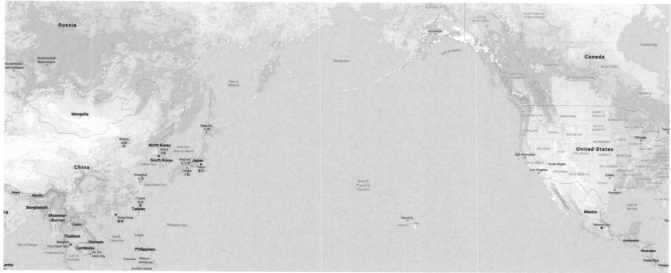

SOURCE: GOOGLE MAPS

Supporting Question 1

Source A: Political map of North America.

https://www.eduplace.com/ss/maps/pdf/n_america_pol.pdf

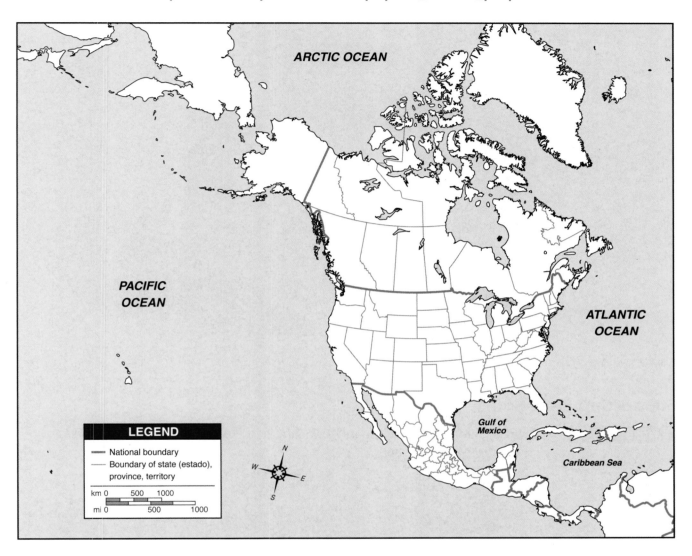

Supporting Question 1

Source B: "South up" world map.

https://commons.wikimedia.org/wiki/File:Seven_continents_world_upside_down.svg

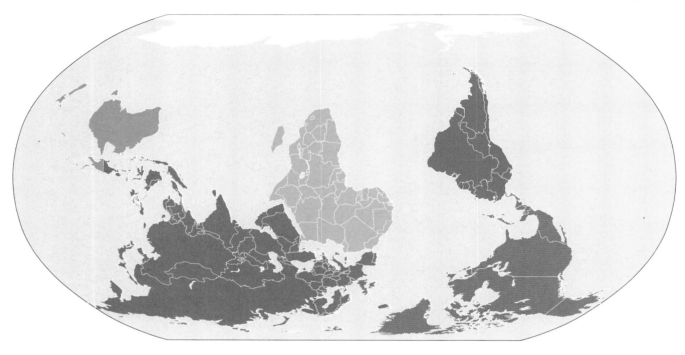

Supporting Question 1

FEATURED SOURCE   Source C: Map of the Korean Peninsula.

SOURCE: GOOGLE MAPS

Supporting Question 1

FEATURED SOURCE Source D: Population density map of South Korea.

http://sedac.ciesin.columbia.edu/downloads/maps/grump-v1/grump-v1-population-density/kordens.jpg

POPULATION DENSITY, 2000

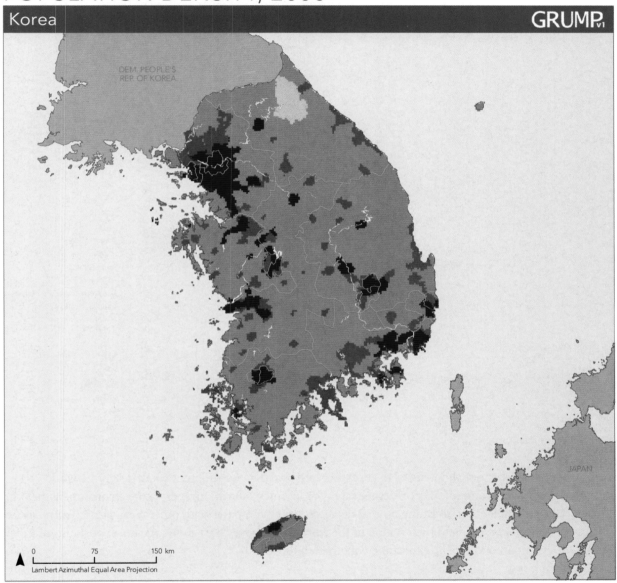

Korea   GRUMP v1

0   75   150 km
Lambert Azimuthal Equal Area Projection

Global Rural-Urban Mapping Project

Persons per km²		Boundaries
☐	0	—— Country
☐	1 - 5	—— Admin. 1
☐	6 - 25	
☐	26 - 250	
☐	251 - 1,000	
■	1,001 +	

Population density measures the number of persons per square kilometer of land area. The data are gridded at a resolution of 30 arc-seconds.

Note: National boundaries are derived from the population grids and thus may appear coarse.

Supporting Question 2

FEATURED SOURCE Source A: Gapminder Mapping Tool: Data on Different Countries.

https://www.gapminder.org/

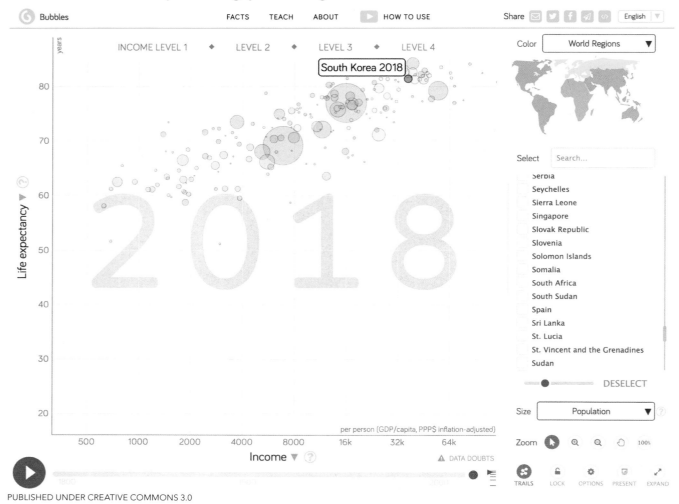

PUBLISHED UNDER CREATIVE COMMONS 3.0

The Gapminder mapping tool allows users to compare statistical data for different countries in the world. Gapminder offers a wide range of data on demography, economics, education, energy, the environment, health, and infrastructure. Readers can examine how a selected country compares with others on a particular measure. Countries are colored according to their region of the world. The above chart shows the life expectancy of inhabitants of South Korea compared to the life expectancy of other countries.

Supporting Question 2

FEATURED SOURCE Source B: Political map of Southeast Asia.

https://www.google.com/maps/place/Korea

SOURCE: GOOGLE MAPS

FEATURED SOURCE Source C: Historical map of Korean Peninsula (1730 C.E.).

https://www.loc.gov/resource/g7900.ct003255/

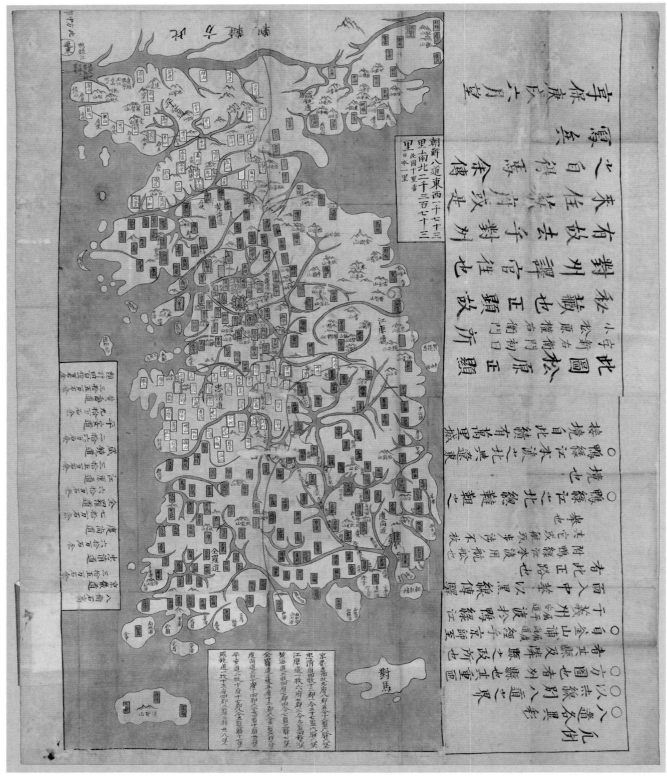

Source D: Map of major Korean rivers.

https://www.revolvy.com/page/List-of-rivers-of-Korea

MAJOR RIVERS OF KOREA

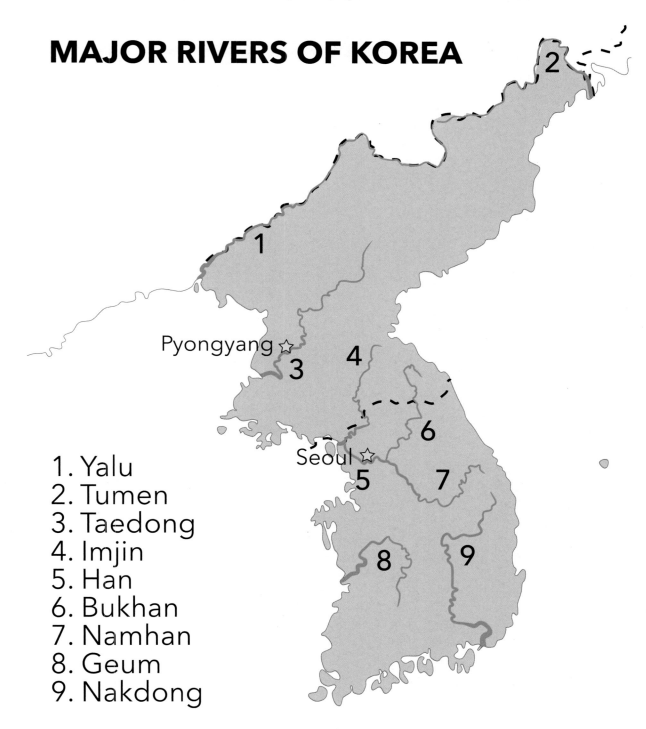

1. Yalu
2. Tumen
3. Taedong
4. Imjin
5. Han
6. Bukhan
7. Namhan
8. Geum
9. Nakdong

CHAPTER 4

Whose Voices are Heard in History?

Elaine Alvey and Kathy Swan

WHOSE VOICES ARE HEARD IN HISTORY?

C3 Framework Indicator	**D2.His.3.3-5.** Generate questions about individuals and groups who have shaped significant historical changes and continuities. **D2.His.16.3-5.** Use evidence to develop a claim about the past.
Staging the Compelling Question	Examine a photograph of a Korean War monument from the National Mall. Consider the race, gender, age, and nationality of the people memorialized. https://www.nps.gov/kowa/index.htm

UNDERSTAND			ASSESS
SUPPORTING QUESTION 1	**SUPPORTING QUESTION 2**	**SUPPORTING QUESTION 3**	**SUPPORTING QUESTION 4**
Whose experiences are recognized in Korean War monuments?	What role did U.S. soldiers of color play in the Korean War?	What contributions did U.S. women make to the Korean War?	Why are some voices omitted in the telling and honoring of history?
FORMATIVE PERFORMANCE TASK	**FORMATIVE PERFORMANCE TASK**	**FORMATIVE PERFORMANCE TASK**	**FORMATIVE PERFORMANCE TASK**
Create a list of the groups of people you see in the monument.	Create a table organizing examples of contributions that people of color made in the Korean War.	Identify two quotes from U.S. women regarding their roles and positions in, and contributions to, the Korean War.	Write a one-paragraph summary of each of these articles' claims and the evidence they provide.
FEATURED SOURCES	**FEATURED SOURCES**	**FEATURED SOURCES**	**FEATURED SOURCES**
Source A: Washington State Memorial **Source B:** New Jersey State Memorial **Source C:** Image, Harry S. Truman at a war memorial in St. Joseph, Missouri	**Source A:** Oral history, Congressman Charles Rangel **Source B:** Images and text from the Patriot Nations exhibit, National Museum of the American Indian **Source C:** Fact sheet, African Americans in the Korean War	**Source A:** Oral history, Voelia "Jean" Thompson **Source B:** Oral history, Mary Reid	**Source A:** Excerpt from the article "Whitewashing the Past" **Source B:** Excerpt from the article "Army Removes Cloud Over Black Korean War Unit"

Summative Performance Task	**ARGUMENT** Construct an argument (e.g., detailed outline, poster, or essay) that discusses the compelling question using specific claims and relevant evidence from historical sources while acknowledging competing views.
Taking Informed Action	**ACT** Create an oral history project to contribute to the Korean War Veterans Digital Memorial (KWVDM) archives that adds to the diversity of the collection.

Overview
Inquiry Description

This inquiry leads students through an investigation of the Korean War by investigating the compelling question "Whose voices are heard in history?" through the evaluation of oral histories, newspaper articles, photographs, and monuments. The formative performance tasks build on knowledge and skills through the course of the inquiry and help students identify points of view that are either present or missing in historical narratives. Students create an evidence-based argument about why some voices are left out of history.

It is important to note that some knowledge of historical events and ideas is necessary for this inquiry. Thus, students should have been introduced to the ideas of historical perspectives and points of view prior to completing the inquiry.

This inquiry is expected to take four to five 30-minute class periods. The inquiry time frame could expand if teachers think their students need additional instructional experiences (i.e., supporting questions, formative performance tasks, and featured sources). Teachers are encouraged to adapt the inquiries in order to meet the requirements and interests of their particular students. Resources can also be modified as necessary to meet individualized education programs (IEPs) or Section 504 plans for students with disabilities.

Structure of the Inquiry

In addressing the compelling question—"Whose voices are heard in history?"—students work through a series of supporting questions, formative performance tasks, and featured sources in order to construct an argument supported by evidence while acknowledging competing perspectives.

STAGING THE COMPELLING QUESTION
In staging the compelling question—"Whose voices are heard in history?"—teachers may prompt students by looking at the Korean War Monument on the National Mall in Washington, DC, and considering who is included. Who is memorialized in this monument? If students lack grounding in the idea of historical perspectives, teachers may also lead students through an activity to challenge them to consider that history is subjective rather than objective, and that some voices and experiences have been more highly valued than others.

SUPPORTING QUESTION 1

The first supporting question—"Whose experiences are recognized in Korean War monuments?"—has students identify the groups of people present in memorials of the Korean War by considering the genders, races, nationalities, and ages of the people depicted in the monument. The formative performance task asks students to list these groups of people and notice trends. The featured sources for this question are all images of Korean War monuments; the selected images represent geographic diversity and the wide variety of stylistic choices. Students analyze the memorial on Washington, DC's National Mall in the staging activity, so these sources look at state and local Korean War memorials. Source A is an image of the Washington State Korean War Memorial and a description of the artist's design rationale. Source B is an image of the New Jersey State Korean War Memorial and Source C is an image of President Harry S. Truman in front of a memorial in St. Joseph, Missouri. These are just a small sampling of the hundreds of Korean War memorials around the country and the world.

SUPPORTING QUESTION 2

To answer the second supporting question—"What role did U.S. soldiers of color play in the Korean War?"—students create a table organizing examples of contributions made by people of color during the war. Building on the resources from the previous supporting question, the featured sources here provide students with additional materials that allow them to construct an understanding of the vast and important contributions of Native American and African American soldiers to U.S. efforts in Korea. Featured Source A is an oral history from Congressman Charles Rangel, who describes his service during the Korean War, the segregation and racism he experienced in the service, and his life after the service. Featured Source B consists of information and images from the Patriot Nations exhibit at the National Museum of the American Indian (Smithsonian Institution, Washington, DC). Featured Source C is a fact sheet about the many contributions made by African Americans during the Korean War.

SUPPORTING QUESTION 3

The third supporting question—"What contributions did U.S. women make to the Korean War?"—asks students to identify at least three quotes from women regarding their roles, positions, and contributions to the war. In addition to the previous featured sources, the sources here highlight the voices and experiences of women during the war. Sources A and B are oral histories collected from two women—Voelia "Jean" Thompson and Mary Reid—who served in the military and made unique contributions during the Korean War. Students could also review the oral history of Shirley Toepfer, which is presented in the next chapter as Source C for Supporting Question 1.

SUPPORTING QUESTION 4

The fourth supporting question—"Why are some voices omitted in the telling and honoring of history?"—asks students to summarize the claims and evidence presented in two featured sources that present reasons and explanations for the exclusion of certain people in the telling of history. Featured Source A is an excerpt from Bob Peterson's article, "Whitewashing the Past." Featured Source B is an excerpt from Michael Kilian's *Chicago Tribune* article about a Black infantry unit that was recently restored to full honor based on a review that showed their failure on the battlefield during the Korean War was the result of institutional racism.

SUMMATIVE PERFORMANCE TASK

At this point in the inquiry, students have examined which groups of people are most frequently recognized in public memorials, identified important contributions of U.S. women and soldiers of color during the Korean War, and begun to explore why some voices and experiences might be omitted in the telling and honoring of history.

Students should be able to demonstrate the breadth of their understanding and their ability to use evidence from multiple sources to support their claims. In this task, students construct an evidence-based argument using multiple sources to answer the compelling question "Whose voices are heard in history?" Students' arguments will take a variety of forms, including a detailed outline, poster, or essay.

Students' arguments will vary, but could include any of the following:

- The voices of women and people of color are largely excluded from history.

- The voices of white men are highlighted throughout history.

- The voices of the "victors" are recorded more than any other voices.

- The American perspective is captured in the dominant narrative of history.

- The experiences of Native Americans are usually omitted from the telling of history.

To extend their arguments, students might rewrite their U.S. history textbook's passage about the Korean War in a way that is inclusive of a greater number of people and stories, suggest additions or changes that expand our understanding of the diverse groups of people who contributed greatly to the U.S. efforts in the Korean War, or design a Korean War monument that also values the contributions of women and people of color.

Students have the opportunity to take informed action by drawing on their understandings of the voices included and excluded in the dominant narratives in history. To understand, students can explore the Korean War Veterans Digital Memorial (KWVDM) Interview Initiative and identify local veteran groups or other community members who are Korean War veterans. To assess the issue, students can explore the diversity of veterans, including their nationalities, genders, and races, and identify ways in which students can contribute to the initiative. To act, students can create an oral history project to contribute to the KWVDM archives, adding to the diversity of the collection.

Staging the Compelling Question

FEATURED SOURCE Source A: Images of the Korean War Monument on the National Mall, Washington, DC.

There are many images of the Korean War monument that can be used to stage the compelling question. Students should review the different images at https://www.nps.gov/kowa/learn/ and consider who is being memorialized in each image.

Supporting Question 1

Source A: Washington State Korean War Memorial

As an example of Korean War memorials in different states, students can review the Washington State Korean War Memorial at: https://des.wa.gov/services/facilities-leasing/capitol-campus/memorials-and-artwork/korean-war-memorial

Montana artist Deborah Copenhaver Fellow's idea was chosen for the memorial after a three-month design competition. Fellow's father is a Korean War veteran. Students can examine the design rationale for her memorial. Her two-ton bronze statue features three weary-faced men of different nationalities huddled around a pile of sticks in the rain, with one soldier attempting to light a fire. Behind the figures fly 22 flags, representing each of the nations that joined the U.S. in the war effort. In front of the bronze statue are stone tablets with the names of those Washington soldiers killed in battle. The memorial describes the war as "The Forgotten War."

The Washington State Korean War memorial site offers the following useful summary of the war:

> The Korean War began on June 25, 1950, when the North Korean Army invaded the Republic of (South) Korea. Three days later, President Harry Truman ordered U.S. troops to help defend South Korea. Soon, and for the first time in history, the United Nations created a United Nations Command to repel the attack. Approximately 1,500,000 American troops served in Korea during the conflict, nearly 53,000 of whom lost their lives. A total of 580,000 United Nations troops were killed, and 1.6 million communist (North Korean and Chinese) soldiers were killed or wounded.

FEATURED SOURCE   Source B: Image of the New Jersey Korean War Memorial

ROREM / SHUTTERSTOCK.COM

As another example of a state memorial, students can examine the New Jersey Korean War Memorial in Atlantic City at http://www.kwva.org/memorials/nj/p_mem_nj.htm. The main statue in the foreground ("The Mourning Soldier") is 12 feet tall. At the back, under an eternal flame, is a granite wall inscribed with the names of 822 New Jerseyans killed or missing in action during the war.

Supporting Question 1

FEATURED SOURCE Source C: Image, President Harry S. Truman standing for photo during a visit to the war memorial in St. Joseph, Missouri, September 26, 1953.

https://www.trumanlibrary.org/photographs/view.php?id=57945

HARRY S. TRUMAN LIBRARY & MUSEUM

Supporting Question 2

FEATURED SOURCE Source A: Oral history interview in which Congressman Charles Rangel shares his reflections on serving in the Korean War.

https://koreanwarlegacy.org/interviews/congressman-charles-rangel

Charles Rangel was born on June 11, 1930 in Harlem, New York. At the age of 17, he enlisted in the military as a way to help support his family. During the Korean War, he served in the 2nd Infantry Division. He was awarded the Bronze Star and Purple Heart for leading a group of men out of a Chinese encirclement at Kunu Ri. He famously has noted that being injured that day was the worst day of his life, and that he has "never had a bad day since." Charles Rangel is best known for his life after the military in which he served in the U.S. House of Representatives representing New York from 1971-2017.

In this oral history, Rep. Rangel describes how although the military was desegregated in 1948, the reality of segregation was still present during his military career. Students can learn more about his experience in the Korean War by listening to his oral history.

Supporting Question 2

FEATURED SOURCE Source B: Images and text from the exhibit "Patriot Nations: Native Americans in Our Nation's Armed Forces," National Museum of the American Indian at the Smithsonian Institution.

http://nmai.si.edu/static/patriot-nations/korea-vietnam.html#korea

The American forces who fought in Korea included approximately 10,000 American Indian soldiers. Considered a "police action" because Congress issued no formal declaration of war, the Korean War was nevertheless bloody and brutal. Some 33,739 American soldiers died in battle, including 194 Native Americans.

Students can learn about the experiences of Native American Soldiers in the Korean War by visiting an online exhibit of the Smithsonian Museum of the American Indian at https://americanindian.si.edu/static/patriot-nations/korea-vietnam.html#korea. One of the soldiers mentioned in the exhibit is Master Sergeant Woodrow Wilson Keeble (Eastern Sioux, 1917–1982). He was a veteran of World War II and the Korean War. For his actions in combat, he received the Distinguished Service Cross, the Silver Star, the Bronze Star, two Purple Hearts, and the Combat Infantryman Badge. In 2007, his Distinguished Service Cross was posthumously upgraded to the Medal of Honor for his bravery during the Korean War. Another soldier mentioned in the exhibit is John Emhoolah (Kiowa/Arapaho, b. 1929) who was one of five brothers who served in the military. Upon his return from the Korean War, he became active in the fight to restore Native Nations' treaty rights.

Students can reflect on a statement by Chester Nez (Diné [Navajo]), a World War II and Korean War veteran: "People ask me, 'Why did you go? Look at all the mistreatment that has been done to your people.' Somebody's got to go, somebody's got to defend this country. Somebody's got to defend the freedom. This is the reason why I went."

Supporting Question 2

FEATURED SOURCE

Source C: Fact sheet on African Americans in the Korean War, "The Beginnings of a New Era for African-Americans in the Armed Forces" (excerpt).

FACT SHEET

The Beginnings of a New Era for African-Americans in the Armed Forces

BUDDIES AID A WOUNDED MAN OF THE 24TH INFANTRY REGIMENT, 25TH DIVISION AFTER A BATTLE 10 MILES SOUTH OF CHORWON.

African Americans served in all combat and combat service elements during the Korean War and were involved in all major combat operations, including the advance of United Nations Forces to the Chinese border. In June 1950, almost 100,000 African Americans were on active duty in the U.S. armed forces, equaling about 8 percent of total manpower. By the end of the war, probably more than 600,000 African Americans had served in the military.

Changes in the United States, the growth of Black political power and the U.S. Defense Department's realization that African Americans were being underutilized because of racial prejudice led to new opportunities for African Americans serving in the Korean War. In October 1951, the all-Black 24th Infantry Regiment, a unit established in 1869, which had served during the Spanish-American War, World War I, World War II, and the beginning of the Korean War, was disbanded, essentially ending segregation in the U.S. Army. In the last two years of the Korean War throughout the services, hundreds of Blacks held command positions, were posted to elite units such as combat aviation, and served in a variety of technical military specialties. Additionally, more Blacks than might have done so in a segregated military chose to stay in the armed forces after the war because of the improved social environment, financial benefits, educational opportunities, and promotion potential.

Distinguished Service

African American servicemen distinguished themselves in combat during the ground battles with the North Korean Army and in the air war over Korea. On July 21, 1950, a battalion combat team commanded by Lieutenant Colonel Samuel Pierce, Jr., composed of three infantry companies and an engineer company, recaptured Yech'on.

The action, which received national attention in the United States, was considered the first significant successful offensive operation by the U.S. Army in the war. Captain Charles Bussey, commander of the engineer company, was awarded the Silver Star for having prevented a flanking operation by a North Korean battalion during the battle. Bussey's platoon-size unit killed more than 250 enemy soldiers. Captain Bussey's bravery inspired his regiment and exemplified the preparedness and leadership capabilities of African American soldiers.

Heroes in the Air War

In 1950, the Air Force had 25 Black pilots in integrated fighter squadrons led by Captain Daniel "Chappie" James, Jr., who was assigned to the 36th Squadron, 5th Air Force. Captain James was an exceptional fighter pilot who often flew his F-86 Sabre jet on dangerous, unarmed reconnaissance missions behind enemy lines—a task reserved for a select group of the most able and trusted flyers. James flew 101 combat missions in Korea and earned the Distinguished Flying Cross before being reassigned stateside. In July 1951, he became the first African American in the Air Force to command a fighter squadron.

Second Lieutenant Frank E. Peterson, Jr., was the first Black Marine Corps pilot. Peterson flew 64 combat missions before the war ended. He earned the Distinguished Flying Cross and six Air Medals in the final months of the Korean War.

Ensign Jesse L. Brown, the Navy's first African American fighter pilot to die in combat, was shot down while providing close-air support for units of the 7th Marines during the Chosin Reservoir breakout in December 1950. Brown was posthumously awarded the Distinguished

Flying Cross for performing dangerous combat actions that resulted in his fatal crash. In March 1972, Brown's widow christened a Knox-class ocean escort ship the USS *Jesse Brown*.

African Americans Who Gave Their Lives During the Korean War

Of the more than 600,000 African Americans who served in the armed forces during the Korean War, it is estimated that more than 5,000 died in combat. Because casualty records compiled by the services in the 1950s did not differentiate by race, the exact number of Blacks killed in action cannot be determined.

Numerous African Americans were awarded medals including the Distinguished Service Cross, Silver Star, and Bronze Star for service during the Korean War. Two African Americans, Private First Class William Thompson and Sergeant Cornelius Charlton were posthumously awarded the Medal of Honor. Thompson was killed in action on August 2, 1951, at a critical juncture in the 8th Army's attempt to stop the North Korean Army's southward movement. Charlton displayed extraordinary heroism in rallying his platoon to continue its assault on a hill near Chipo-ri, just north of the 38th parallel.

The Korean War changed the face of the American military. African Americans served side by side in the same units with service members of all races and were afforded the opportunity to lead in combat.

In June 1950, almost 100,000 African Americans were on active duty in the U.S. armed forces, equaling about 8 percent of total manpower. In the Army, 9.7 percent of active duty service members were Black, including 72,000 enlisted men and approximately 1,200 officers. In the Air Force, 4.4 percent of active duty personnel were Black, including 21,000 enlisted men and 300 officers. About 6,000 African Americans, or about 3 percent of personnel, served in the Navy and Marine Corps. By the end of the war, probably more than 600,000 Blacks had served in the armed forces.

Supporting Question 3

Source A: Oral history interview with Voelia "Jean" Thompson, a Korean War Air Force veteran who was later stationed in Japan as a top-secret Central officer.

http://koreanwarlegacy.org/interviews/voelia-jean-thompson

USED WITH PERMISSION FROM THE KOREAN WAR LEGACY PROJECT

Voelia Jeanne Thompson was born in 1926 in Duncan, Oklahoma. After graduating from Oklahoma Agricultural and Mechanical College, she went to work for a newspaper in Texas. The yearning to travel led her to apply for a Women in the Air Force (WAF) commission. After working at bases in Oklahoma, Illinois, and Hawaii, she was stationed in Japan and served as a top secret central officer. Her duties included delivering top secret documents. In 1961, she left her commission and had a family. Students can learn more about her experience in the Korean War by listening to her oral history.

Supporting Question 3

Source B: Oral history interview with Mary Reid, a Korean War veteran who served as an Army nurse in Korea during the war.

http://koreanwarlegacy.org/interviews/mary-reid

USED WITH PERMISSION FROM THE KOREAN WAR LEGACY PROJECT

Mary Reid was born in Pittsburgh, Pennsylvania on April 9, 1927. Although she grew up poor and during the Great Depression, she speaks fondly of her time playing with neighborhood kids. After graduating from high school, she enrolled in the Nurses Cadet Corps, which was housed at the Western Pennsylvania Hospital of Nursing. After graduating in 1948, she volunteered to serve as a nurse in Korea. She looks back on her service with great pride and is happy that South Korea has developed into what it is today. Students can learn more about Mary's experience in the Korean War by listening to her oral history.

Supporting Question 4

Source A: Article, "Whitewashing the Past" (excerpt), Bob Peterson, from *Rethinking Schools*, (www.rethinkingschools.org), Vol. 23, No. 1, Fall 2008

Ever since the Civil Rights Movement, there has been grassroots pressure by educators and community activists to change the textbooks used in U.S. schools. Progress was made. Blatantly racist references to Africa and favorable comments about slavery were eliminated, photos were diversified, and stories of famous African Americans and women started appearing, if not in the main text, at least in scattered sidebars.

Despite improvements, however, most mainstream social studies textbooks remain tethered to sanitized versions of history that bore students and mislead young minds. This was brought home to me earlier this year [in 2008] when I examined the social studies textbook series being considered for adoption by the Milwaukee Public Schools. The books were from the dwindling constellation of large textbook publishers—Houghton Mifflin, Macmillan McGraw-Hill, and Scott Foresman.

In keeping with state social studies standards, the 5th-grade textbooks in each series focus on United States history. Even though publishers make claims about being "multicultural" and honoring our nation's "diversity," none of the 5th-grade United States history textbooks—even those exceeding 800 pages—examines the role of racism in U.S. history or even mentions the word "racism." In two textbooks, the word "discrimination" doesn't even appear. Nor do the texts tell students that any United States president ever owned slaves, even though 12 of the first 18 did, and all of the two-term presidents up until Lincoln owned and sold human beings.

As my colleagues and I examined the books more closely, a picture emerged that profoundly disturbed us. With important issues like racism, inequality, and conquest falling through the cracks of the historical narrative, there is little reason to recount the resistance to those types of oppression. There are occasional terse summations of resistance, but the bountiful history of people working together, crossing racial boundaries, and building social movements to make this country more democratic and just is omitted. Instead, history is more often viewed from the vantage point of the rich and powerful, the conquerors.

Supporting Question 4

FEATURED SOURCE Source B: Article, "Army Removes Cloud Over Black Korean War Unit" (excerpt), Michael Kilian, Washington Bureau, *Chicago Tribune*, April 30, 1996.

http://articles.chicagotribune.com/1996-04-30/news/9604300190_1_24th-infantry-regiment-white-units-official-army-report

WASHINGTON — An all-black U.S. Army infantry regiment, disbanded and singled out for cowardice and unreliability in the Korean War, has had its honor restored in an official Army report made public Monday.

Its failures were directly attributable to neglect, inferior white leadership and institutional racism, according to the study, which is based on 400 interviews and took nine years to complete.

CHAPTER 5

What Is the Best Way to Remember History?

Elaine Alvey and Kathy Swan

WHAT IS THE BEST WAY TO REMEMBER HISTORY?

C3 Framework Indicator	**D2.His.4.3-5.** Explain why individuals and groups during the same historical period differed in their perspectives.
Staging the Compelling Question	Discuss why people study history, and create a class-generated list of the tools available for learning about and remembering history.

SUPPORTING QUESTION 1	SUPPORTING QUESTION 2	SUPPORTING QUESTION 3
What are some of the ways the Korean War has been memorialized?	How do we remember all the parts of history?	How does the memory of history help us make better choices today?
FORMATIVE PERFORMANCE TASK	**FORMATIVE PERFORMANCE TASK**	**FORMATIVE PERFORMANCE TASK**
Create a T-chart that lists the ways the Korean War has been memorialized and the strengths and weaknesses of each of these types of memorials.	Make a list of some of the parts of history we forget to include in memorials, textbooks, or stories about history.	Create a claim about how history might help us learn to make better choices in the future.
FEATURED SOURCES	**FEATURED SOURCES**	**FEATURED SOURCES**
Source A: Image bank: Korean War Veterans Memorial, Washington, DC **Source B:** Memorial songs about Korea, "There's Peace in Korea" and "Forgotten Men" **Source C:** Videotaped oral history interviews with two Korean War veterans	**Source A:** Illustrated oral history, War and Children **Source B:** Veterans Affairs fact sheet, "Korean War Exposures" **Source C:** Article about an unexpected benefit of the demilitarized zone for wildlife species, *The Guardian* **Source D:** Article about bias and discrimination against African American soldiers in the Korean War, *Chicago Tribune*	**Source A:** Article, "Why Study History?," Humboldt University, Berlin, Germany **Source B:** Article about the importance of preserving heritage sites, GoUNESCO

Summative Performance Task	**ARGUMENT** What is the best way to remember history? Construct an argument (e.g., detailed outline, poster, or essay) that addresses the compelling question using specific claims and relevant evidence from both historical and current sources.
	EXTENSION Conduct research on historical markers and monuments in your town and answer the question, "What stories do they tell?"
Taking Informed Action	**UNDERSTAND** Working with a team, discuss how history can teach important lessons and support us in making better choices in the future. Discuss your examples from Supporting Question 3.
	ASSESS Identify problems in your community that might be solved by learning a lesson from history.
	ACT Create a memorial design that you would put in your town to help your community learn from history, so that it can make the best choices for the future.

Overview
Inquiry Description

This inquiry leads students through an investigation of the ways we remember history, including a variety of memorials, and consideration of the omissions in our collective memory. By investigating the compelling question "What is the best way to remember history?" students evaluate and explore a variety of types of memorialization, omissions in our collective memory, and the possible ways that historical memory can help people make better contemporary choices. The formative performance tasks build on knowledge and skills through the course of the inquiry and help students identify and compare some of the ways history is memorialized and remembered. Students create an evidence-based argument about the best ways to engage in the process of preserving the past.

It is important to note that little prerequisite knowledge of historical events and ideas is necessary for this inquiry, although skills for decoding historical and new source texts are helpful.

This inquiry is expected to take three to four 30-minute class periods. The inquiry time frame might expand if teachers think their students need additional instructional experiences (i.e., supporting questions, formative performance tasks, and featured sources). Teachers are encouraged to adapt the inquiries to meet the requirements and interests of their particular students. Resources can also be modified as necessary to meet individualized education programs (IEPs) or Section 504 plans for students with disabilities.

Structure of the Inquiry

In addressing the compelling question "What is the best way to remember history?" students work through a series of supporting questions, formative performance tasks, and featured sources in order to construct an argument supported by evidence while acknowledging competing perspectives.

STAGING THE COMPELLING QUESTION

In staging the compelling question, "What is the best way to remember history?" teachers may prompt students with two tasks. First, students should discuss with a partner some of the reasons why studying and remembering history might be important. Second, the class should work together to generate a list of sources for remembering history. These might include textbooks, songs, murals in the school, family stories, community or national memorials, and posters or other works of art. Creating a rich list of sources for remembering history will provide students with scaffolding for creating an argument about which ways of remembering history are best.

SUPPORTING QUESTION 1

The first supporting question, "What are some of the ways the Korean War has been memorialized?" has students consider a variety of memorializations and examine the strengths and weaknesses of each type of memorial. The formative performance task asks students to create a T-chart with this information. The featured sources for this question represent three ways the Korean War has been memorialized. The class list generated in the staging activity demonstrates that this is not an exhaustive list, but a small selection for student consideration. Featured Source A is a captioned image bank from the Korean War

Veterans Memorial on the National Mall in Washington, DC. Featured Source B is a pair of war-era songs and their lyrics commemorating the Korean War and honoring its veterans. Featured Source C is a pair of interviews with Korean War veterans providing oral histories. In addition to the content of the oral histories, this featured source allows students to see that the acts of recording, and then listening to, the lived experiences of veterans are also forms of memorialization.

SUPPORTING QUESTION 2

For the second supporting question, "How do we remember all the parts of history?" students will identify some of the hard, unflattering, or simply forgotten parts of history that are sometimes omitted from our collective memory. For the formative performance task, students are asked to list parts of history that are often forgotten. In addition to the resources from Supporting Question 1, the featured sources here provide students with additional materials that allow them to summarize and identify some of the omissions in our remembrances. Featured Source A is a set of documents about the experiences of children in war, including several photos (these are not graphic, and are appropriate for young students) and a videotaped oral history on the orphanages and starvation faced by children during and after the Korean War. Featured Source B is a Veterans Affairs fact sheet on some of the occupational and environmental hazards faced by soldiers and veterans. Featured Source C is an article from *The Guardian* that briefly discusses the adaptation of wildlife to the Korean demilitarized zone. Featured Source D is an article from the *Chicago Tribune* that addresses the racism experienced by soldiers of color during and after the Korean War. Additional instructional resources on the experiences of African American soldiers in the war and the racism they encountered can be found in the Korean War Legacy Project's archives (https://koreanwarlegacy.org).

SUPPORTING QUESTION 3

The third supporting question, "How does the memory of history help us make better choices today?" asks students to consider the ways in which we can learn from the past. In addition to the previous featured sources for this inquiry, the sources for this task explore the reasons to study and preserve history. Featured Source A is an article from the Department of History at Humboldt University in Berlin, Germany outlining the reasons to study history. Featured Source B is an article from GoUNESCO listing the reasons to preserve history. The formative performance task asks students to create a claim about how remembering history might help us make better choices today and in the future.

SUMMATIVE PERFORMANCE TASK

At this point in the inquiry, students have examined some of the ways history is typically memorialized, identified topics and people who are sometimes omitted from the dominant narrative, and considered the uses of memorials in helping us make better choices now and in the future.

Students should be able to demonstrate the breadth of their understanding and their ability to use evidence from multiple sources to support their claims. In this task, students construct an evidence-based argument using multiple sources to answer the compelling question "What is the best way to remember history?" Students' arguments could take a variety of forms, including a detailed outline, poster, or essay.

Students' arguments will vary, but could include any of the following:

The best way to remember history is to…

- Listen to the stories of people who were there.

- Create art or music to memorialize the experiences of people who were there.

- Read about history in books.

- Create posters and share them widely in your town or via the internet.

- Talk about the experiences of people, places, and issues that have been omitted.

To extend students' arguments, teachers may have students conduct research on local historical markers and monuments and write about their value. Teachers could provide the prompts: What story does this memorial tell us about history? What can we learn from this monument that is helpful today? What monuments might be missing from our town?

Students have the opportunity to take informed action by drawing on their understanding of collective memory and historical memorialization. To understand, small groups of students can discuss how history can teach important lessons and support us in making better choices now and in the future. Discuss examples from Supporting Question 3 and collectively add examples that are both personal and historical. To assess the issue, students can identify problems in the community that might be solved by learning a lesson from history. To act, students can create a memorial design that could be put in their town to help their community learn from history and make the best choices for the town's future.

Source A: Image bank with captions, Korean War Veterans Memorial, National Mall, Washington, DC

http://www.koreanwarvetsmemorial.org/the-memorial

CAROL M. HIGHSMITH

THE MEMORIAL

The Korean War Veterans Memorial is located near the Lincoln Memorial on the National Mall in Washington, D.C. It was dedicated on July 27, 1995. The Memorial was designed and financed by private contributions and erected under the auspices of the Korean War Veterans Memorial Advisory Board composed of Korean War veterans appointed by President Reagan. The memorial commemorates the sacrifices of the 5.8 million Americans who served in the U.S. armed services during the three-year period of the Korean War. The War was one of the most hard fought in our history. During its relatively short duration from June 25, 1950 to July 27, 1953, 36,574 Americans died in hostile actions in the Korean War theater. Of these, 8,200 are listed as missing in action or lost or buried at sea. In addition, 103,284 were wounded during the conflict. The Memorial consists four main parts: the statues, the Mural Wall, the Pool of Remembrance, and the United Nations Wall.

THE STATUES

The 19 stainless steel statues were sculpted by Frank Gaylord of Barre, Vermont, and cast by Tallix Foundries of Beacon, New York. They are approximately seven feet tall and represent an ethnic cross-section of America. The advance party has 14 Army, three Marine, one Navy, and one Air Force members. The statues stand in patches of juniper bushes and are separated by polished granite strips, which give a semblance of order and symbolize the rice paddies of Korea. The troops wear ponchos partially covering their weapons and equipment. The ponchos seem to blow in the cold winds of Korea.

RICHARD CAVALLERI

THE MURAL WALL

The Mural Wall was designed by Louis Nelson of New York City and fabricated by Cold Spring Granite Company, in Cold Spring, Minnesota. The muralist, sculptor, and architect worked closely to create a two-dimensional work of art adjacent to the three-dimensional statues. The wall consists of 41 panels extending 164 feet. More than 2,400 photographs of the Korean War were obtained from the National Archives. They were enhanced by computer to give a uniform lighting effect and enlarged to the desired size. The mural, representing those forces supporting the foot soldier, depicts Army, Navy, Marine Corps, Air Force and Coast Guard personnel and their equipment. The etchings are arranged to give a wavy appearance in harmony with the layout of the statues. The reflective quality of the Academy Black Granite creates the image of a total of 38 statues, symbolic of the 38th Parallel and the 38 months of the war. When viewed from afar, it also creates the appearance of the mountain ranges of Korea.

THE POOL OF REMEMBRANCE

The Memorial has a reflective pool at the far terminus of the memorial site. It encircles the Freedom Is Not Free Wall and Alcove at the base of which are numerically listed the cost of the war to soldiers in terms of KIA (Killed in Action), WIA (Wounded in Action), MIA (Missing in Action), and POWs (Prisoners of War). The pool is encircled by a walkway along which benches are located.

THE UNITED NATIONS WALL

To the left of the Mural Wall is a walkway on which engraved markers list the 22 nations that contributed troops to the United Nations' efforts in the Korean War.

Supporting Question 1

Source B: Two memorial songs about Korea: Rosetta Tharpe, "There's Peace in Korea" (1953), and Don Reno and Red Smiley, "Forgotten Men" (1956)

"THERE'S PEACE IN KOREA"

PERFORMED BY SISTER ROSETTA THARPE
RECORDED IN 1953
WRITTEN BY ROSETTA THARPE AND M. ASHER

I'm so glad at last, there's peace in Korea
Yes, I'm so glad at last, there's peace in
Korea
Don't you know, I'm so glad at last, there's
peace in Korea
Because President Eisenhower has done just
what he said

We're hoping there will be no more misery,
and no more sadness
No no no no no no dying, there'll be, in the
land
Hope we'll have happiness, and joy, and
peace of mind
Because we know God has made this world
And made it for the good and kind

I'm seeing all you mothers, now don't you
weep and moan
I know that you are glad because your sons
are comin' home
Note to wise, sisters and brothers, you can
wipe your cheery eyes
Because, sure as I'm singing, the sun has
begun to shine

[repeat first verse twice]

RETRIEVED FROM: HTTPS://WWW.HISTORYONTHENET.COM/
AUTHENTICHISTORY/1946-1960/2-KOREA/3-MUSIC/19530000_
THERES_PEACE_IN_KOREA-SISTER_ROSETTA_THARPE.HTML

HTTPS://CREATIVECOMMONS.ORG/LICENSES/BY/3.0/

"FORGOTTEN MEN"

PERFORMED BY DON RENO AND RED SMILEY
RECORDED AUGUST 27, 1956

Forgotten men who lie asleep across the
ocean waves
Who fought and died for the flag that waves
across their lonely graves

The flag still waves so proud and free across
our land today
Let's not forget the boys who died across the
watery spray

Forgotten men who lie asleep across the
ocean waves
Who fought and died for the flag that waves
across their lonely graves

Her picture hangs upon the wall but their
names are not mentioned back home
As the years go by our memories dim, we
forget our loved ones are gone

Forgotten men who lie asleep across the
ocean waves
Who fought and died for the flag that waves
across their lonely graves

RETRIEVED FROM: HTTPS://WWW.HISTORYONTHENET.COM/
AUTHENTICHISTORY/1946-1960/2-KOREA/3-MUSIC/19560827_
FORGOTTEN_MEN-DON_RENO-RED_SMILEY.HTML

HTTPS://CREATIVECOMMONS.ORG/LICENSES/BY/3.0/

Supporting Question 1

Source C: videotaped oral histories of Korean War veterans Shirley Toepfer and Doris Porpiglia

https://koreanwarlegacy.org/interviews/shirley-toepfer

USED WITH PERMISSION FROM THE KOREAN WAR LEGACY PROJECT

Shirley Toepfer was born in Petersburg, Michigan, in 1931. Raised on a farm, she learned to work hard and persevere. After going to college at Eastern Michigan University for two years, she left school and enlisted in the Army. During basic training, she was identified as someone who might be helpful to counter-intelligence, and she was sent to Ft. Holabird in downtown Baltimore, Maryland, where she worked with the counter-intelligence detachment. After four years, she was forced to leave the service due to pregnancy. She would eventually have four children with her first husband, and after raising the children, would work as a mail carrier. She looks back at the Korean War with great admiration for the people who fought for democracy.

https://koreanwarlegacy.org/interviews/doris-b-porpiglia

USED WITH PERMISSION FROM THE KOREAN WAR LEGACY PROJECT

Although Doris Porpiglia was shy while in high school in Amsterdam, New York, she enlisted in the Army and earned the rank of Private First Class. She served in the army post office, for which she received training in Indianapolis, Indiana. She describes the role of women during the Korean War and the importance of obtaining the skills they would later use in other jobs after the war. Doris was in charge of communicating with the commanding officers to determine the assignment location of both incoming and discharged soldiers. Wherever they were going, she made sure that they would receive their mail. After serving in the Army from 1951-1953, she returned to Amsterdam, but she decided to seek work in Syracuse, New York, where she lives today. Doris believes that the role that women played during the Korean War paved the way for the future involvement of women in the military.

Students can learn more about Shirley and Doris' experiences in the Korean War and the role that women played in the war by listening to the oral history recorded by the Korean War Legacy Foundation.

Supporting Question 2

Source A: Oral History Interview with Bill Scott on War's Impact on children

https://koreanwarlegacy.org/interviews/bill-scott

USED WITH PERMISSION FROM THE KOREAN WAR LEGACY PROJECT

Bill Scott was one of sixty-two students at his local high school in Oklahoma who were called to serve in the National Guard when the Korean War broke out. He completed his basic training at Camp Polk in Louisiana before he was assigned as a Squadron Leader to the 179th Infantry Regiment, 45th Infantry Division. Having landed near Seoul in 1952, it was only two days before he and his regiment were sent to the front lines where he saw action at Old Baldy, Pork Chop Hill, T-Bone, and Hasacal. Bill Scott describes the conditions on the hills he defended and the lives that were lost, expressing pride for having served in a country that is so thankful for U.S. efforts.

When Bill Scott arrived in Seoul, the soldiers were given 4-5 days worth of rations. After seeing starving children with or without parents, the soldiers fed the babies with their own food rather than watch them starve. Soldiers knew that they had to take care of the kids and they were proud to have done it.

Students can learn more about Bill's experience in the Korean War and the impact of war on children by listening to the oral history recorded by the Korean War Legacy Foundation.

Supporting Question 2

FEATURED SOURCE Source B: United States Department of Veterans Affairs, "Korean War Exposures"

https://www.publichealth.va.gov/exposures/wars-operations/korean-war.asp

Korean War Exposures

Korean War (June 25, 1950-July 27, 1953)

Veterans who fought in the Korean War may have been exposed to the following hazards that carried potential health risks.

 Cold Injuries
Possible health problems from cold-weather injuries, especially during the Chosin Reservoir campaign

 Noise
Harmful sounds from guns, equipment, and machinery that is often experienced during service

 Occupational Hazards
Exposures from working with chemicals, paints, and machinery during service

This fact sheet defines and discusses the primary, known health hazards of serving in the Korean War, and details causes, health implications, symptoms, treatments, and benefits available to veterans.

FEATURED SOURCE   Source C: Lisa Brady, "How Wildlife Is Thriving in the Korean Peninsula's Demilitarized Zone," *The Guardian*, April 13, 2012

https://www.theguardian.com/environment/2012/apr/13/wildlife-thriving-korean-demilitarised-zone

In this article, the author examines an unintended benefit of establishing a zone without human inhabitants—an accidental sanctuary in which wildlife thrives.

The forces that lock humans out of the DMZ have allowed other species to thrive. Could a remnant of violent conflict become the symbol of a greener, more peaceful future?

Lisa Brady for China Dialogue, part of the Guardian Environment Network

A thin green ribbon threads its way across the Korean Peninsula. Viewed from space, via composite satellite images, the winding swath clearly demarcates the political boundary between the Republic of Korea (ROK) [South Korea] and the Democratic People's Republic of Korea (DPRK) [North Korea]. Its visual impact is especially strong in the west, where it separates the gray, concrete sprawl of Seoul from the brown, deforested wastes south of Kaesong. In the east, it merges with the greener landscapes of the Taebaek Mountain Range and all but disappears.

From the ground, the narrow verdant band manifests as an impenetrable barrier of overgrown vegetation enclosed by layers of fences topped by menacing concertina wire and dotted with observation posts manned by heavily armed soldiers. That a place so steeped in violence still teems with life seems unimaginable. And yet, the Demilitarized Zone, or DMZ, is home to thousands of species that are extinct or endangered elsewhere on the peninsula. It is the last haven for many of these plants and animals and the center of attention for those intent on preserving Korea's rich ecological heritage.

Once known as the "land of embroidered rivers and mountains," the Korean Peninsula has experienced almost continual conflict for over 100 years, resulting in a severely degraded natural environment. International competition for control over the peninsula's resources left Korea in a precarious position at the start of the twentieth century. The Japanese occupation between 1905 and 1945 brought with it radically increased exploitation of mineral and other resources, resulting in massive deforestation, pollution, and general environmental decline.

▲ Manchurian cranes with their distinctive black and white feathers fly low over fields in Chulwon valley, just south of the Korean Demilitarized Zone. Photograph: AP

Since at least the 1940s, deforestation for fuel wood and clearing for agricultural land has caused significant erosion of the area's mountains and hills and contributed to the siltation of its rivers, streams and lakes. The 1950 to 1953 war raged across the entire peninsula, subjecting it to widespread devastation that destroyed cities, roads, forests and even mountains. And, in the 1960s and 1970s, unchecked industrialization further undermined the peninsula's ecological health, causing air, water, and soil pollution.

The relative health of the DMZ now stands in stark contrast to the failing ecosystems in both North and South Korea.

Created in 1953 during tense armistice negotiations, Korea's DMZ is at once one of the most dangerous places on Earth and one of the safest. For humans, its thousands of landmines and the millions of soldiers arrayed along its edges pose an imminent threat. But the same forces that prevent humans from moving within the nearly 400 square miles of the DMZ encourage other species to thrive. Manchurian or red-crowned cranes and white-naped cranes are among the DMZ's most famous and visible denizens. Nearly 100 species of fish, perhaps 45 types of amphibians and reptiles, and more than 1,000 different insect species are also supposed to exist in the protected zone.

Scientists estimate that more than 1,600 types of vascular plants and more than 300 species of mushrooms, fungi, and lichen are thriving in the DMZ. Mammals such as the rare Amur goral, Asiatic black bear, musk deer, and spotted seal inhabit the DMZ's land and marine ecosystems. There are even reports of tigers, believed [to have been] extinct on the peninsula since before Japanese occupation, roaming the DMZ's mountains.

Much of the biodiversity in the DMZ is speculative, extrapolated from spotty scientific studies conducted in the Civilian Control Zone (CCZ) that forms an additional protective barrier along the DMZ's southern edge. Approximate though these studies are, the DMZ's ecological promise is great enough to spur many people to action.

Supporting Question 2

FEATURED SOURCE | Source D: Article by Michael Kilian about the racism African American soldiers faced in the Korean War, "Army Removes Cloud Over Black Korean War Unit," *Chicago Tribune*, April 30, 1996

http://articles.chicagotribune.com/1996-04-30/news/9604300190_1_24th-infantry-regiment-white-units-official-army-report

An all-black U.S. Army infantry regiment, disbanded and singled out for cowardice and unreliability in the Korean War, has had its honor restored in an official Army report made public Monday [April 29, 1996].

Its failures were directly attributable to neglect, inferior white leadership, and institutional racism, according to the study, which is based on 400 interviews and took nine years to complete.

Supporting Question 3

FEATURED SOURCE Source A: Professor Thomas Mergel, Department of History, Humboldt University, Berlin, Germany, "Why Study History?" (excerpt, September 2018)

https://www.geschichte.hu-berlin.de/en/studying-history/why-study-history/why-study-history

WHY STUDY HISTORY?

[When asked why anyone should study history,] many would say, "Because we can learn things from history that can help us in the future." But is that really true? Of course!

History does not simply prepare us for a future that is identical to the past. Instead, it makes us aware of the fact that we must be open to anything and everything that might await us.

The first reason: Because history has already taught us that nothing stays the same. When studying history, we don't just discuss how different politics and economics have become. Instead, we look into how, throughout history, bodies, feelings, and social values have varied. Almost everything today that we take for granted—or even consider natural—turns out, upon further inspection, to have developed over the course of time and could, therefore, change again. Thus, the study of history teaches us that all things are historical and, therefore, have the potential of becoming something different overnight.

The second reason: When we study the monks of the Middle Ages, the American settlers of the 18th century, or the Athenians [of ancient eras], we learn how diverse humans and societies can be. What was natural for those people is now foreign to us. Students of history are given an ethnological view of the world, a wide panorama of the potential diversity of people and cultures.

Viewing the world in such a way allows us to put the present day into perspective. It gives us the impression that our current way of life is not so "normal" or "natural." It encourages us to be open to change. History does not simply prepare us for a future that is identical to the past. Instead, it makes us aware of that fact that we must be open to anything and everything that might await us.

EXCERPTED AND USED WITH PERMISSION FROM: DEPARTMENT OF HISTORY, HUMBOLDT-UNIVERSITÄT ZU BERLIN

Supporting Question 3

FEATURED SOURCE

Source B: GoUNESCO, "5 Reasons Why We Should Preserve Heritage Sites" (excerpt), in which some of the reasons to preserve historically significant places are discussed, GoUNESCO website, July 5, 2014.

https://www.gounesco.com/why-preserve-heritage-sites

GoUNESCO is a citizen-led, UNESCO-supported umbrella of initiatives that make heritage more engaging. Here are four reasons offered by GoUNESCO for preserving historically significant places.

WHY SHOULD WE PRESERVE HERITAGE SITES?

Heritage sites and memorials are symbols of history. They are a representation of the past, and sometimes it becomes hard to understand why, exactly, we need to spend the time, energy, and money to preserve heritage sites. Are they really important in our contemporary world? Apparently, they are!

1. The evolution of human consciousness is a continuous process.

History here serves as a laboratory, and the past serves as [contextualization] to understand regional laws and social structures. This understanding helps our progress toward an ideal society.

2. We are not born capable of judging fairly and wisely.

However, learning about various cultures helps us to be good global citizens and improve our critical and analytical thinking skills.

3. Every historical site has an important story to tell.

These stories have inspired many people to strengthen their convictions and their commitment to fight injustice and oppression.

4. Heritage sites are our connection to the past.

Heritage sites are living monuments and records of [important] happenings, and this is our real connection to our past.

CHAPTER 6

What If **You** Were the Historian?

Elaine Alvey and Kathy Swan

WHAT IF YOU WERE THE HISTORIAN?

C3 Framework Indicator	**D2. His.6.3-5**. Describe how people's perspectives shaped the historical sources they created. **D2.His.10.3-5**. Compare information provided by different historical sources about the past.
Staging the Compelling Question	Teachers will have students watch the first 35 seconds of an awareness test video and individually record their telling of the event in the video. Next, rewatch the entire video as a class and lead a whole-class discussion of the variations of historical telling based on perspective and viewpoint. Introduce the concept of evaluating historical documents for perspective during this discussion. The concept of corroborating or contradicting documents and sources with each other should also be introduced to students in this staging activity.

SUPPORTING QUESTION 1

What do these two primary source documents say about this historical event or topic?

FORMATIVE PERFORMANCE TASK

Using the graphic organizer in Appendix A, identify the narratives and facts shared by these primary source documents about the racism experienced by Korean War soldiers. Appendices B and C provide additional tools for the evaluation of primary sources.

FEATURED SOURCES

Source A: Oral history, John E. Saxton
Source B: Oral history, Dottie Harris

SUPPORTING QUESTION 2

How can you corroborate or contradict this with an additional primary source document from the archival materials?

FORMATIVE PERFORMANCE TASK

Using the Korean War Veterans Digital Memorial Project, corroborate or contradict the information shared in the featured sources of Supporting Question 1. Use the graphic organizer in Appendix A to help organize your thoughts.

FEATURED SOURCES

Source A: Link to Korean War Memorial Digital Archives
Source B: Link to Interactive Memory Bank

Summative Performance Task	**ARGUMENT** Construct an argument that evaluates the primary source documents to create a one-paragraph summary of the topic or event.
	EXTENSION Students can further explore the memory bank and primary source documents and discuss with a partner the strengths and weaknesses of genres of primary source information in order to explore the question, "How do we know what really happened in history?"

Overview
Memory Bank Exploration Activity

To explore the memory bank, teachers and students will watch two to three video clips on a common topic or event and then explore the archives in order to find documents that corroborate or contradict ideas and events shared in the oral history clip. Appendix A is an organizational framework for this inquiry-driven activity. The memory bank can be retrieved at https://koreanwarlegacy.org/chapters and additional archival material can be found at http://www.kwvdm.org/collection.php?p=artifact. Appendices B and C provide additional tools for evaluating primary sources.

1. In order to use the document set provided here as one possible variation, students should watch the two videos related to the racism experienced by Korean War soldiers, noting the experiences and facts shared in each oral history. These two oral histories have some corroborating and some contradictory ideas and perspectives.

2. Students will then explore the online archival database to find materials that corroborate or contradict these narratives. The graphic organizer provided in Appendix A is designed to help students in this process.

This activity can be altered to allow for greater flexibility in terms of topic or event, in order to meet the content requirements or technological resources available. For example, teachers could select a particular topic or event for students to explore, or students could explore the memory bank to select and then research a topic that interests them, as outlined in the following two steps.

1. In a student-driven activity, teachers should encourage students to navigate the oral history memory bank independently or in small groups, using key terms they find interesting. The memory bank has been coded for easy searches that allow students to identify common topics or events, and includes a list of tags for possible areas of exploration.

2. Students then search through the digital archive of primary sources for documents, photos, or artifacts that help them build a greater understanding of this topic, seeking to corroborate or contradict their findings from the oral history clips.

Staging the Compelling Question

To stage the activity, teachers may prompt students with an Awareness Test video that invites students to retell an event portrayed in the video. An online search for "Awareness Test" will identify suitable tests. The British website https://www.awarenesstest.co.uk offers several different tests of this kind.

For class purposes we recommend the Awareness Test at https://www.youtube.com/watch?v=oSQJP40PcGI or https://www.youtube.com/watch?v=hcUkdPxkJHU. Teachers should show students the first 35 seconds of the video, then pause it and ask students to spend a few minutes writing down their retelling of the event in the video. When students are finished writing, teachers should replay the entire video for students to view together as a class.

After the class views the entire video, teachers will want to lead a class discussion on the variations of historical tellings based on perspective and viewpoint, introducing the concept of evaluating historical documents for perspective through the variety of perspectives provided by students' individual re-tellings of the video. Students' re-tellings of the events in the video will vary from individual to individual, providing a starting point for this discussion.

This class discussion should include:

1. An introduction to the idea of *corroboration* as a tool historians use to gather the best information about historical events and the experiences of people who lived through them.

2. An introduction to the idea that our *perspective* is changed by what we can actually see (as in the case of the video) as well as the era and our own or the participants' nation of origin, belief system, and historical perspective. Historical documents almost always present some perspectives more thoroughly and/or favorably than others.

SUPPORTING QUESTION 1

Students listen to two oral histories that discuss racism in the armed forces during the Korean War, in order to answer the first supporting question: What do these primary sources say about this historical event or topic? In the first oral history, John Saxton recalls the attitude of an army commander who had a low regard for African American troops. In the second oral history, Dottie Harris, a woman who enlisted in the U.S. Air Force in 1951, shares her memory of racist attitudes expressed by Air Force personnel during the War.

SUPPORTING QUESTION 2

The second supporting question asks students to corroborate or contradict the evidence used to answer Supporting Question 1 with an additional primary source document from archival materials. To obtain a suitable document, they examine primary sources from the Korean War Veterans Digital Memorial Project, using the graphic organizer in Appendix A to help organize their thoughts.

SUMMATIVE PERFORMANCE TASK

At this point in the inquiry, students have examined a variety of primary sources on a topic of interest and attempted to find corroborating and/or conflicting evidence in documents discovered while searching archival material. In this summative performance task, students should evaluate the evidence they have gathered and engage in writing a paragraph that summarizes the event or the topic of racism as experienced by soldiers in the Korean War.

Students should be able to demonstrate the breadth of their understanding and their ability to use evidence from multiple sources to support their claims. In this task, students construct an evidence-based evaluation utilizing multiple sources, and use their historical thinking and evaluative skills to build an interpretation of an event or topic from history.

As an extension, students may dig deeper into the digital archives to explore the question, "How do we know what really happened in history?" This extension activity asks students to evaluate the strengths and limitations of different types of historical primary source documents. Scaffolds and examples of this can be found in Appendix C.

Students' answers to this extension question will vary. Some possible answers include:

■ Historians must corroborate information using a variety of sources in order to know what really happened in history.

■ We must consider the voices that have been omitted from historical documents in order to understand what *really* happened in history; these voices include those of women, people of color, and children.

■ We must select the right sources for our purpose and carefully evaluate the point of view of each.

■ We can't always know what really happened in history, but historians develop theories based on the best evidence available.

This inquiry is expected to take four to five 30-minute class periods. The inquiry time frame could expand if teachers think their students need additional instructional experiences (i.e., supporting questions, formative performance tasks, and featured sources). Teachers are encouraged to adapt the inquiries in order to meet the requirements and interests of their particular students. Resources can also be modified as necessary to meet individualized education programs (IEPs) or Section 504 plans for students with disabilities.

Supporting Question 1

FEATURED SOURCE Source A: Oral history interview with John E. Saxton, an African American who served in the Army during the Korean War, Korean War Legacy Project.

https://koreanwarlegacy.org/interviews/john-e-saxton

USED WITH PERMISSION FROM THE KOREAN WAR LEGACY PROJECT

John Saxton was born in 1929 in Kearneysville, West Virginia. His father fought in World War I and suffered lifelong effects as a result of being gassed in the war. Two of John's brothers served in World War II, and two other brothers served in Korea. As it was difficult to find work in his town, John enlisted in the army in 1949. He did basic training at Fort Dix and was sent to Fort Hood to train for an armored artillery battalion. He was assigned to the Third Infantry Division and participated in many battles in Korea, including the Pusan Perimeter and Chosin Lakes.

In this oral history, he recounts how a commander of the X Corps held African American troops in Korea in low regard based on his belief that African American soldiers had performed poorly during a World War II campaign in Italy. His story about carry-over racism from World War II is accessible on the Korean War Legacy Foundation website.

Supporting Question 1

FEATURED SOURCE Source B: Oral history interview with Dottie Harris, a veteran who witnessed racism while serving in the Air Force from 1951-1952.

https://koreanwarlegacy.org/interviews/dottie-harris

USED WITH PERMISSION FROM THE KOREAN WAR LEGACY PROJECT

Dottie Harris was born in Verona, Pennsylvania, in October 1931. She was living with her grandparents and working as a cashier at Krogers when she decided to enlist into the United States Air Force on January 31, 1951 in Pittsburgh, Pennsylvania. She was stationed at James Connally Air Force Base in Waco, Texas in May 1951. Before she was discharged in July 1952, she served as an Airman 1st Class sergeant, specializing as an officer in Personnel Flying Training.

The Air Force was the first branch of the service to be fully integrated. However, Dottie Harris tells of a specific incident where she witnessed African American men in service being called names, and because she sat and had dinner near them, she was also called names. Some white men in the service thought that there should be neither Blacks nor women in Air Force uniform.

Supporting Question 2

FEATURED SOURCE Students should corroborate or contradict the evidence used to answer Supporting Question 1 with an additional primary source document from archival materials.

https://koreanwarlegacy.org/chapters

http://www.kwvdm.org/collection.php?p=artifact

To obtain a suitable document, they can examine the memory bank at https://koreanwarlegacy.org/chapters and additional archival material at http://www.kwvdm.org/collection.php?p=artifact. They should use Appendix A to help organize their thoughts.

Appendix A: Comparing and Corroborating Primary Source Documents (Organizer)

Topic or event: _____

Perspective of oral history #1:	Perspective of oral history #2:

What corroborating or contradicting evidence can be found in the archives?

What really happened? How do you know? Use evidence from the primary sources to support your claim.

Appendix B: Viewing Guide for Oral History Videos (Scaffolding Tool)

Oral histories are a tool used to document people's experiences. Listen to one of the veterans talking about his or her life in the oral histories provided, and reflect on these questions as you listen.

Veteran's Name: _____

Military Service Start Year: _____ **Millitary Service End Year:** _____

What are two facts you learned about history from listening to this oral history? 1. 2.	What surprised you most about this story? What did you find most interesting? Why?
What are two facts you learned about this person and their perspective from listening to this oral history? 1. 2.	What remaining questions do you have about the historical events discussed or the people who experienced them?

Appendix C: Tools for Exploring Strengths and Weaknesses of Primary Sources

STRENGTHS AND WEAKNESSES OF PRIMARY SOURCES

Type of Primary Source	Strengths	Weaknesses
IMAGES A visual record obtained through photography or painting.	• Visual record of a particular moment in time. • Conveys a variety of details about people, places, objects, and events. • Conveys information about everyday life and behavior that is best communicated in visual terms (hair and clothing styles, interior design). • Sometimes provides evidence of the photographer or painter's attitude. • Important to the study of people who did not leave many written records. • Can stimulate the personal involvement of the viewer. • Can be used to stimulate the memory of an oral history informant.	• Not a complete or objective source: the image that serves as the lasting record may not equate directly with the reality of the event itself. • The relationship of the photographer or painter to his or her subject is not always clear. • One must consider the bias or perspective of the photographer or painter, including: – the choice of subject – the choice of timing – the subject matter that a person present at the event chose to record. – whether the people or objects have been manipulated by the photographer or painter. • The people, place, date, and photographer or painter are often not identified. • The emotions and thoughts of those involved often are not evident. • Information from this kind of source is often suggestive rather than definitive; photographs and paintings must be studied in conjunction with other evidence, i.e., documents and oral histories, to determine if the information is unusual or part of a larger pattern.
Type of Primary Source	**Strengths**	**Weaknesses**
DOCUMENTS Printed or written materials that communicate and record information. Examples include: diaries; letters; birth/death, or marriage certificates; deeds; contracts, constitutions, laws, court records; tax records; census records; wills, inventories; treaties; report cards; medical records; passenger lists; passports; visas; naturalization papers; military enlistment or discharge papers.	• Provide information on the "who, what, where, when, why, and how" of an event. • Provide written, printed, or graphic information. • Purpose of the communication or transaction is often clear. • May indicate the social and economic status of the author. • May offer insight into the emotional state of the author. • Can stimulate the personal involvement of the reader.	• May not be a thoroughly objective source. • Generally a verbal, rather than a visual record. • May not consider other views or perspectives on the same event(s). • The identity of the author may be unclear (especially true in the case of government documents). • The author is usually no longer living and therefore cannot be consulted for verification. • May be difficult to read: handwriting may be difficult to decipher; words or phrases may be unfamiliar and their meanings may have changed over time. • Documents must be evaluated in conjunction with other evidence to determine whether they present information that is exceptional or conforms to previously established patterns

CONTINUED ON PAGE 84

| ORAL HISTORY
The record of an individual's (informant's) reminiscences, accounts, and interpretations of the past in his or her own spoken words obtained through planned interview(s) and preserved through the use of audio or video tape, film, or written transcription. | • Personalizes history by recording an individual's remembrances (or opinions) about her or his life or an event in which he or she was involved.
• Provides information about a topic or time period that may otherwise lack documentation in written or archival records.
• Often conveys emotion clearly.
• Contains spontaneity and candor not always present in a personally written account.
• May contain unusual dialect or speech patterns.
• Often the informant is living and may be consulted for clarification or additional information. | • The memory of the informant is fallible.
• The informant may intentionally or unintentionally distort the event or her or his role in the event, thereby compromising the record's validity.
• The informant may be reluctant to discuss certain topics, resulting in an inaccurate or incomplete record.
• The informant's testimony may not be consistent from one interview to the next.
• The bias, objective, or the relationship of the interviewer to those being interviewed must be considered.
• The interviewer's questions may intentionally or unintentionally influence the informant's response.
• Unfamiliar words or phrases from another time may not be clarified by informant.
• The bias of the historian or interviewer may be evident in the edited version of the interview(s).
• Oral history is the mutual creation of the historian and the person being interviewed: the historian creates the topic or problem to be studied, and the informant provides the information.
• Oral histories must be evaluated in conjunction with other evidence to determine whether they present information that is exceptional or conforms to previously established patterns. |

PART TWO

MIDDLE-LEVEL INQUIRIES

CHAPTER 7

Teaching about Korea in the **Middle School**

Kathy Swan, John Lee, and S.G. Grant

The Korean War has never held a prominent position in the middle school curriculum. But with history courses more typical in grades 6-8, the opportunities for sustained study of the conflict between North Korean and United Nations troops are more readily apparent than in the elementary school curriculum.

The expanding curriculum sequence that holds sway in many elementary schools fades after grade five. The middle school social studies curriculum, by contrast, is far more open-ended.[1] History courses focused on the United States or the world dominate, but some states insert conventional geography courses, world cultures courses, and general social studies courses. Considerable variation also occurs in the history courses. "World history" could mean a focus on ancient civilizations, on the Eastern hemisphere, or on global history at large. United States history courses show a similar content range. In some states, the focus is on the early history of the country up to Reconstruction, while in other states Reconstruction is the first topic in a more contemporary study of the U.S. past.

Regardless of the particular curriculum topics and the sequence in which those topics are presented, the typical middle school social studies curriculum affords opportunities for teachers and their students to engage in rich investigations of the Korean War and the possibilities for a more peaceful relationship between North Korea and the United States. The four inquiries presented in this section look at the wartime implications for children, the role of media in societies during times of peace and war, the meaning of sacrifice, and the powerful importance of words to shape human events. As in the elementary section, the four inquiries here are both academically rigorous and relevant to students' lives.

In this section, we offer a brief overview of the four middle school-level inquiries that make up this section of the book.

Chapter 8 (How Does War Affect Children?) highlights a topic likely to be of considerable interest to middle school students. Although students have lots of ideas about warfare, state curriculums and school textbooks rarely focus on the lived experiences of war's most vulnerable populations. The brutal conditions that soldiers face merit considerable attention, but the powerful effects of war can be felt well beyond the battlefield.[2]

The questions, tasks, and sources in this inquiry put evidence of war's far-reaching implications in front of middle school students. Drawing from photographs of Korean children and the testimonies of U.S. soldiers, students learn about the various ways that children in the Korean countryside experienced the conflict. Students can then use the knowledge they have built to examine the fates of children in two contemporary situations— in Syria and in South Sudan. At the completion of the inquiry, students are well positioned to craft a range of evidence-based arguments in response to the compelling question, "How does war affect children?"

Although this inquiry builds out from the Korean War, teachers could insert it in a range of places throughout the middle school curriculum. Apart from a section on the Cold War, one could imagine a teacher deciding to conduct this inquiry before introducing World War I or World War II in a world history course or before a unit on the Vietnam War in a

U.S. history course. It's also possible to imagine a teacher using the inquiry as one of a set of investigations early in the school year as a way to encourage students to think about how the past and the present may not be so dissimilar.

In similar fashion, the compelling question in Chapter 9—"How can media be used to influence others?"—might be used at the beginning of the school year to set a context for students' academic studies to come. The role of media—in its historic and contemporary forms—has often been an overlooked element of social studies courses.[3] Allowing students to examine this cultural dimension in the fall could pay off nicely as students encounter various examples throughout the school year.[4]

The "Media" inquiry, like the "Children" inquiry, uses the Korean War as a pivot point. Students first examine how the media was used and abused during the Korean conflict. But then the inquiry turns toward the present and the ways that media are used to promote or quash some perspectives, free discussion, and democratic ideals.

Teachers who want to highlight the full scale of warfare might consider pairing Chapters 8 and 10. As noted above, Chapter 8 asks students to consider the many ways that war can impact the lives of children; Chapter 10 pushes them to compare the impact of warfare on soldiers and the wider civilian population. The compelling question behind the inquiry in Chapter 10—"What does it mean to sacrifice?"—highlights one of the common conjunctions between combatants and civilians: the pervasiveness of sacrifice.

When examining the role of warfare in human society, students can be expected to focus on the common sense notion of the sacrifices made by soldiers advancing or defending a cause. The books, movies, and stories they see and hear typically emphasize the front-line tragedies experienced by the troops. Often left undescribed are the tragedies experienced by civilians in war zones. If students are to fully understand the complexity of war, they need to move outward from the soldiers' experiences. Through its extensive use of the many oral histories collected in the Korean War Legacy Project (KWLP) archives, this inquiry accomplishes that effort.

The final inquiry in this section emphasizes one other dimension of warfare that students in the middle grades are likely to underappreciate—the role of ideas, ambitions, and values as expressed through words. Military attacks of one sort or other are clear signs of ensuing combat. What students may not understand is the role that words—as expressed through speeches, diplomatic negotiations, declarations, news reports, and the like—can play in the period leading up to conflict.[5]

The compelling question in Chapter 11—"Can words lead to war?"—is an example of a broad-brush question, one that allows teachers and their students to explore a perennial question through a case study.[6] In this instance, the case focuses on the evolving relationship between American presidents and the North Korean leadership. That relationship has been characterized by rhetorical tensions, both big and small, as these two nations try to find a way to coexist. What makes this inquiry unique is that we see these diplomatic tensions playing out in real time today. Media savvy teachers will want to include current events in the inquiry as the U.S.–North Korean relationship continues to evolve.

As with the elementary chapters in Part One, the inquiries in this section exhibit features worth noting.

Readers will notice that the middle school inquiries are far more history directed than those in the elementary section and revolve largely around the Korean War. The first three deal explicitly with the conflict; the fourth is more contemporary in focus, but the underpinnings are directly related to the war between 1950 and 1953.

Focusing on history, however, does not disrupt the balance between content and skills represented in the middle school inquiries. Students continue to learn how to "read" a wide range of disciplinary sources and to understand and consider a wide range of perspectives. Especially prominent in the four inquiries is use of the KWLP oral history library. This resource not only supports the teacher-directed goals of the inquiries, but readers will notice that the "Sacrifice" inquiry encourages students to investigate the archives on their own.

In contrast to many curriculum units on war-related topics, the middle school inquiries focus less on mobilization, troop movements, battles, and won-lost tallies. Instead, they take students deeply into the array of human costs generated by warfare. Also notable is the emphasis on media and the role it can play in both promoting and defusing impulses toward war.

Elevating the function of media is one way that the inquiries in this section speak directly to the lives of students today. Their comfort with the many ways people can communicate ideas ought not to lull teachers into thinking that their students understand and appreciate the trade-offs inherent across media platforms. But building outward from their students' common knowledge and experience should help teachers encourage and support their students' access to the people, ideas, and events profiled. In a different way, notions of sacrifice should prove useful touchstones as students work to recognize and appreciate the complexities of the Korean War. Although few students will have experienced anything like the privations of the Korean populace, the idea of sacrifice will be familiar enough that they should be able to empathize with the military and civilian participants.

One other feature of the middle school inquiries is the varied structure that some of the blueprints exhibit. The "Children" and "Words" inquiries both feature a sequence of three supporting questions, which is typical of many inquiries. The "Media" and "Sacrifice" inquiries, by contrast, have only two supporting questions. The variation plays to the idea that teachers are always pressed for time. Realizing that they can use (and create) shorter, more focused inquiries, should help teachers manage the time pressures they face. Creating curriculum spaces for study of the Korean War will be easier for middle school teachers than for their elementary school peers. The examination of the effect of war on combatants and civilians, with a special focus on children, supports the study of this particular conflict. As we note above, however, the implications of the Korean War can be applied more broadly, and teachers can use the inquiries in this section to explore a wide range of their curricular goals.

NOTES

1. E. W. Ross (Ed.), *The Social Studies Curriculum: Purposes, Problems, and Possibilities*, 3rd ed. (Albany, NY: SUNY Press, 2006).

2. A. Raviv, L. Oppenheimer, and D. Bar-Tal, *How Children Understand War and Peace: A Call for International Peace Education* (Somerset, NJ: John Wiley and Sons, 1999).

3. T. Walker, "The Red Pill: Social Studies, Media Texts, and Literacies," *Learning, Media, and Technology* 35, no. 1 (2010), 1-14.

4. K. Greene, I. Yanovitzky, and A. Carpenter, "A Theory-grounded Measure of Adolescents' Response to Media Intervention," *Journal of Media Literacy Education*, 7, no. 2 (2015), 35-49.

5. S. Casey, *Selling the Korean War: Propaganda, Politics, and Public Opinion in the United States*, 1950-1953 (Oxford, UK: Oxford University Press, 2010); B. Cumings, *The Korean War: A History* (New York: Modern Library, 2011).

6. K. Swan, J. Lee, and S. G. Grant, *Inquiry Design Model: Building Inquiries in Social Studies* (Silver Spring, MD: National Council for the Social Studies and C3 Teachers, 2018).

CHAPTER 8

How Does War
Affect Children?

Mona Al-Hayani and John Lee

Korean children in front of a tank.

	HOW DOES WAR AFFECT CHILDREN?
C3 Framework Indicator	**D2.Civ.14.6-8.** Compare historical and contemporary means of changing societies and promoting the common good.
Staging the Compelling Question	Discuss the effects of war on children by viewing the clip from the Korean War Legacy Foundation where Veteran George Drake describes the evacuation of 950 Korean orphans prior to the Chinese occupation of Seoul.

SUPPORTING QUESTION 1	SUPPORTING QUESTION 2	SUPPORTING QUESTION 3
What were the experiences of Korean children during the Korean War?	What were the experiences of Korean children during the Korean War from the perspective of U.S. soldiers?	What are the human costs of displacement and war?
FORMATIVE PERFORMANCE TASK	**FORMATIVE PERFORMANCE TASK**	**FORMATIVE PERFORMANCE TASK**
Construct the story of a child depicted in the photographs during the Korean War.	Write a paragraph about the experiences of Korean children during the war from the perspective of American soldiers.	Create four historical questions about the human costs of displacement and war to prepare for a guided Socratic Seminar.
FEATURED SOURCES	**FEATURED SOURCES**	**FEATURED SOURCES**
Source A: Photographs of children during the Korean War	**Source A:** Video clip, oral history interview with Charles Buckley **Source B:** Video clip, oral history interview with Everett Kelley **Source C:** Video clip, oral history interview with Andrew Lanza	**Source A:** Video clip, Syrian children describing experiences with war and conflict **Source B:** Video clip, effects of war on children in South Sudan **Source C:** Information from the UN Refugee Agency on the effects of war and global displacement due to war and conflict

Summative Performance Task	**ARGUMENT** How does war affect children? Construct an argument (e.g., detailed outline, poster, or essay) that discusses the compelling question using specific claims and relevant evidence from the sources provided and one other source, while acknowledging competing views.
	EXTENSION Discuss a current refugee/orphan crisis in the context of the summative argument.
Taking Informed Action	**UNDERSTAND** Examine the plight of contemporary refugees and orphans of war, and the effects of their displacement.
	ASSESS Consider what the United Nations, individuals, and non-governmental organizations can do to promote the common good of contemporary refugees and orphans of war.
	ACT Working with a partner, create a short story or picture book portraying how war affects children. Students will share their books with refugees or orphans of war in their schools and community.

Overview
Inquiry Description

This inquiry leads students through an investigation of the consequences faced by children of war, including hunger, displacement, trauma, and the loss of family and stability. By investigating the compelling question "How does war affect children?" students attempt to contextualize the consequences of war on children. The formative performance tasks help students build knowledge and skills through the course of the inquiry as they examine the experiences of Korean children during the war, the role members of the armed forces played in helping these children, and the human costs of displacement and war. Students create an evidence-based argument about Korean children's war-time experiences and members of the armed forces' role in helping the children, and then write historical questions about the human costs of displacement and war to prepare for a guided Socratic Seminar.

Some knowledge of historical events and ideas is a prerequisite for this inquiry. Students should be somewhat familiar with ongoing contemporary refugee crises, but the sources provided should suffice as an introduction to these crises, if necessary.

This inquiry is expected to take four 40-minute class periods. The inquiry timeframe could expand if teachers think their students need additional instructional experiences (i.e., supporting questions, formative performance tasks, and featured sources). Teachers are encouraged to adapt the inquiries in order to meet the requirements and interests of their particular students. Resources can also be modified as necessary to meet individualized education programs (IEPs) or Section 504 plans for students with disabilities.

Structure of the Inquiry

In addressing the compelling question "How does war affect children?" students work through a series of supporting questions, formative performance tasks, and featured sources in order to construct an argument supported by evidence while acknowledging competing perspectives.

STAGING THE COMPELLING QUESTION
In staging the compelling question "How does war affect children?" teachers may prompt students with the video clip from the Korean War Legacy Foundation in which Korean War veteran George Drake describes the evacuation of 950 Korean orphans prior to the Chinese occupation of Seoul.

SUPPORTING QUESTION 1
The first supporting question—"What were the experiences of Korean children during the Korean War?—encourages students to examine the consequences of war on Korean children using photographs from the period. The formative performance task asks students to construct the story of a child depicted in the photographs during the Korean War.

The featured source for this question is a collection of photographs depicting children during the Korean War.

SUPPORTING QUESTION 2

The second supporting question—"What were the experiences of Korean children during the Korean War from the perspective of U.S. soldiers?"—has students expand on their examination of the consequences of war on Korean children. The formative performance task asks students to discuss with a partner and write a paragraph about the experiences of Korean children during the war from the perspective of American soldiers serving in the Korean War.

In addition to the resources from the previous supporting question, the featured sources provide students with additional materials that allow them to gain an understanding of how American soldiers viewed experiences of Korean children during the war. All three featured sources for this question are video clips with veterans of the Korean War from the Korean War Legacy Project. Featured Source A is a clip from an interview with Charles Buckley in which he talks about the suffering of Korean children during the war as well as the ways soldiers tried to help Korean children. Featured Source B is a clip from an interview in which Everett Kelley describes how he tried to help Korean children during the war. Featured Source C is a clip from an interview in which Andrew Lanza discusses the effects of war on Korean children.

SUPPORTING QUESTION 3

For the third supporting question—"What are the human costs of displacement and war?"—students write four historical questions about the human costs of displacement and war to prepare for a guided Socratic Seminar. The questions should reflect a range of thinking about, and engagement with, the topic.

In addition to the resources from the previous supporting questions, the featured sources here provide students with materials that allow them to learn more about other conflicts that have had an impact on children. Featured Source A is a video clip of Syrian children describing their experiences with war and conflict. Featured Source B is a video clip on the effects of war on children in South Sudan. Featured Source C includes information from the UN Refugee Agency on the effects of war and global displacement due to war and conflict.

SUMMATIVE PERFORMANCE TASK

At this point in the inquiry, students have contextualized children's experiences of war, and have examined the human costs of war and displacement.

Students should be able to demonstrate the breadth of their understanding and their ability to use evidence from multiple sources to support their claims. In this task, students construct an evidence-based argument using multiple sources to answer the compelling question "How does war affect children?" Students' arguments will take a variety of forms, including a detailed outline, poster, or essay.

Students' arguments will vary, but could include any of the following:

- War affects children by making them homeless.

- War affects children because they won't have food or clean water.

- War affects children by making them afraid.

To help students extend their arguments, teachers may have students read aloud with a partner a children's story or picture book exploring the contemporary refugee/orphan crisis, and thoughtfully analyze the book in a whole-group discussion.

Students have the opportunity to take informed action by analyzing the effects of war on children. To understand, students can draw on their understandings of the plight of contemporary refugees, orphans of war, and the effects of their displacement. To assess the issue, students should consider what the United Nations, individuals, and/or non-governmental organizations can do to promote the common good of contemporary refugees and orphans of war. To act, students might create a short story or picture book portraying how war affects children, and share these with refugees or orphans of war in their schools or communities.

Staging the Compelling Question

FEATURED SOURCE   Oral history interview with Korean War veteran George Drake, who describes the evacuation of 950 Korean Orphans prior to the Chinese occupation of Seoul, South Korea.

https://koreanwarlegacy.org/interviews/george-drake

USED WITH PERMISSION FROM THE KOREAN WAR LEGACY PROJECT

George Drake enlisted in the Army in June 1950. Trained in Intelligence and Communication, he worked with the soldiers of several United Nations countries during his time in Korea from August 1952 until December 1953. He describes the evacuation of 950 Korean orphans prior to the Chinese occupation of Seoul, and recalls how American soldiers and other Americans supported Korean orphans during the war.

Supporting Question 1

Source A: Images of children of the Korean War from the image bank of the Korean War Legacy Foundation.

http://www.kwvdm.org/detail_artifact.php?no=5099

USED WITH PERMISSION FROM THE KOREAN WAR LEGACY PROJECT

Additional images at:

http://www.kwvdm.org/detail_artifact.php?no=87

http://www.kwvdm.org/detail_artifact.php?no=477

http://www.kwvdm.org/detail_artifact.php?no=1241

http://www.kwvdm.org/detail_artifact.php?no=1248

http://www.kwvdm.org/detail_artifact.php?no=2237

A PICTURE OF A CHILD CARRYING HIS YOUNGER BROTHER ON HIS BACK.
USED WITH PERMISSION FROM THE KOREAN WAR LEGACY PROJECT

A SOLDIER HOLDS A HOMELESS KOREAN BOY WHOM HE AND HIS COMPANY HAD UNOFFICIALLY ADOPTED.
USED WITH PERMISSION FROM THE KOREAN WAR LEGACY PROJECT

Supporting Question 2

Source A: Oral history interview with Charles Buckley, a Korean War veteran, who discusses the suffering of Korean children during the war and the ways in which Buckley and other soldiers tried to help them.

https://koreanwarlegacy.org/interviews/charles-buckley

USED WITH PERMISSION FROM THE KOREAN WAR LEGACY PROJECT

After graduating from high school in Tulsa, Oklahoma, Charles Buckley enlisted in the National Guard in 1947 and was active until November 1948, when he joined the Air Force. He worked toward becoming an Independent Duty Medical Technician, and made his mark in June 1953 working at a hospital training other surgical technicians by using radio to communicate with medical support teams at other operating sites in Korea. During and after his time in Korea, he helped to provide supplies to orphaned children.

Supporting Question 2

Source B: Oral history interview with Everett Kelley, a Korean War veteran, who discusses how he and others helped Korean children during the war.

https://koreanwarlegacy.org/interviews/everett-kelley/#clip-life-impact

USED WITH PERMISSION FROM THE KOREAN WAR LEGACY PROJECT

Everett Kelley was drafted into the military while living in Miami, Florida, and served in Korea after the War. He provides his impressions of Korea, recounts the living conditions he experienced while stationed abroad, and describes the relationship between American and South Korean soldiers during his stay. He believes that if any solution to the Korean conflict were to occur, it would most likely stem from a uniting of both the North and South. His experience sponsoring children in an orphanage greatly impacted his life.

Supporting Question 2

FEATURED SOURCE Source C: Oral history interview with Andrew Lanza, a Korean War veteran, who discusses the effects of war on Korean children.

https://koreanwarlegacy.org/interviews/andrew-lanza

USED WITH PERMISSION FROM THE KOREAN WAR LEGACY PROJECT

Andrew Lanza was studying to be a watchmaker when he decided to enlist because his brother was serving in Korea. He joined the Marines and served in Korea from 1952 to 1953, specializing in artillery and in security. He believes that American students need to learn more about the Korean War and to understand that it was not a police action, as it was described at the time, but a war, not unlike the first and second world wars. He recalls the plight of Korean children, and shares memories of hungry children carrying other children, some of whom were badly injured, on their backs.

Supporting Question 3

FEATURED SOURCE Source A: A video clip from BBC News of Syrian children describing their experiences with war and conflict.

https://www.youtube.com/watch?v=2iz2tNiRpeY

It was very scary

We would hide in barrels and our family would come searching for us.

We no longer dared go out to play.

SOURCE: BBC NEWS

In this video clip, Syrian children describe the effects of war on their lives as they share their personal experiences of deaths and injuries in their families and the destruction of their homes. They reminisce about the days when they used to play games with each other, enjoy their toys, and go to school.

Supporting Question 3

FEATURED SOURCE

Source B: A video clip on the effects of war on children in South Sudan from Aljazeera News.

https://www.aljazeera.com/news/2018/02/south-sudan-war-deprives-children-education-180202120925076.html

SOURCE: ALJAZEERA NEWS

South Sudan has the world's highest proportion of young children not receiving an education. The civil war has seen thousands of people killed and millions displaced. It's also had a major impact on education, with 1.8 million, or 70 percent of school-age children not getting any education. The United Nations says years of war make it difficult for kids to get to school, even in areas not directly affected by fighting.

Supporting Question 3

FEATURED SOURCE

Source C: United Nations High Commissioner for Refugees (the UN Refugee Agency), "Forced Displacement above 68 million in 2017, New Global Deal on Refugees Critical," article on the effects of war and global displacement due to war and conflict, June 19, 2018.

http://www.unhcr.org/en-us/news/press/2018/6/5b27c2434/forced-displacement-above-68m-2017-new-global-deal-refugees-critical.html

FORCED DISPLACEMENT ABOVE 68 MILLION IN 2017, NEW GLOBAL DEAL ON REFUGEES CRITICAL

Wars, other violence and persecution drove worldwide forced displacement to a new high in 2017 for the fifth year in a row, led by the crisis in Democratic Republic of the Congo, South Sudan's war, and the flight into Bangladesh from Myanmar of hundreds of thousands of Rohingya refugees. Overwhelmingly, it is developing countries that are most affected.

In its annual Global Trends report, released today, UNHCR, the UN Refugee Agency, said 68.5 million people were displaced as of the end of 2017. Among them were 16.2 million people who became displaced during 2017 itself, either for the first time or repeatedly – indicating a huge number of people on the move and equivalent to 44,500 people being displaced each day, or a person becoming displaced every two seconds.

Refugees who have fled their countries to escape conflict and persecution accounted for 25.4 million of the 68.5 million. This is 2.9 million more than in 2016, also the biggest increase UNHCR has seen in a single year. Asylum-seekers, who were still awaiting the outcome of their claims to refugee status as of 31 December 2017, meanwhile rose by around 300,000 to 3.1 million. People displaced inside their own country accounted for 40 million of the total, slightly fewer than the 40.3 million in 2016.

In short, the world had almost as many forcibly displaced people in 2017 as the population of Thailand. Across all countries, one in every 110 persons is someone displaced.

"We are at a watershed, where success in managing forced displacement globally requires a new and far more comprehensive approach so that countries and communities aren't left dealing with this alone," said UN High Commissioner for Refugees Filippo Grandi. "But there is reason for some hope. Fourteen countries are already pioneering a new blueprint for responding to refugee situations and in a matter of months a new Global Compact on Refugees will be ready for adoption by the United Nations General Assembly. Today, on the eve of World Refugee Day, my message to member states is: please support this. No one becomes a refugee by choice; but the rest of us can have a choice about how we help."

UNHCR's Global Trends report is released worldwide each year ahead of World Refugee Day (20th June) and tracks forced displacement based on data gathered by UNHCR, governments, and other partners. It does not examine the global asylum environment, which UNHCR reports on separately and which continued in 2017 to see incidents of forced returns, politicization and scapegoating of refugees, refugees being jailed or denied possibility to work, and several countries objecting even to use of the word "refugee."

Nonetheless, the Global Trends report offers several insights, including in some instances into perceived versus actual realities of forced displacement and how these can sometimes be at odds.

Among these is the notion that the world's displaced are mainly in countries of the Global North. The data shows the opposite to be true—with fully 85 percent of refugees in developing countries, many of which are desperately poor and receive little support to care for these populations. Four out of five refugees remain in countries next door to their own.

Large-scale displacement across borders is also less common than the 68 million global displacement figure suggests. Almost two thirds of those forced to flee are internally displaced people who have not left their own countries. Of the 25.4 million refugees, just over a fifth are Palestinians under the care of UNRWA [the United Nations Relief and Works Agency]. Of the remainder, for whom UNHCR is responsible, two thirds come from just five countries: Syria, Afghanistan, South Sudan, Myanmar and Somalia. An end to conflict in any one of these has the potential to significantly influence the wider global displacement picture.

Two other insights from Global Trends are that most refugees live in urban areas (58 per cent), not in camps or rural areas; and that the global displaced population is young–53 per cent are children, including many who are unaccompanied or separated from their families.

As with the number of countries producing large-scale displacement, the number of countries hosting large numbers was also comparatively few: Turkey remained the world's leading refugee hosting country in terms of absolute numbers with a population of 3.5 million refugees, mainly Syrians. Lebanon meanwhile hosted the largest number of refugees relative to its national population. In all, 63 percent of all refugees under UNHCR's responsibility were in just 10 countries.

Sadly, solutions for all this remained in short supply. Wars and conflict continued to be the major drivers with little visible progress towards peace. Around five million people were able to return to their homes in 2017 with the vast majority returning from internal displacement, but among these were people returning under duress or to fragile contexts. Due to a drop in the number of resettlement places on offer, the number of resettled refugees was down by over 40 per cent at around 100,000 people.

USED WITH PERMISSION FROM UNHCR, THE UN REFUGEE AGENCY. ADDITIONAL UNHCR INFORMATION ABOUT WORLD REFUGEES IS ACCESSIBLE AT HTTP://WWW.UNHCR.ORG/GLOBALTRENDS2016/

CHAPTER 9

How Can Media Be Used to **Influence Others**?

Mona Al-Hayani and John Lee

The front of a leaflet spread by airplane encouraging North Koreans to surrender to the United Nations. Joseph Horton obtained it in December 1952 while he was in a frontline position.

HOW CAN MEDIA BE USED TO INFLUENCE OTHERS?

C3 Framework Indicator	**D2.His.4.6-8. Analyze** multiple factors that influenced the perspectives of people during different historical eras.
Staging the Compelling Question	Explore the uses of media on the battlefield during the Korean War by viewing a U.S. military video.

SUPPORTING QUESTION 1	SUPPORTING QUESTION 2
How was media used and misused during the Korean War?	How is media used and misused in contemporary society, politics, and war?
FORMATIVE PERFORMANCE TASK	**FORMATIVE PERFORMANCE TASK**
Make a T-chart listing uses and misuses of media during the Korean War.	Expand on the T-chart by including additional uses and misuses of media in contemporary society, politics, and war.
FEATURED SOURCES	**FEATURED SOURCES**
Source A: Oral history, Charles Gaush **Source B:** Oral history, Norman Renouf **Source C:** Media artifacts (leaflets) used on Korean War battlefields	**Source A:** Video clip, How Does Fake News Become News? **Source B:** Article (interview transcript) on how social media is reshaping contemporary conflict **Source C:** Selected slides from Lee Rainie's presentation, "The New Age of Politics and Media"

Summative Performance Task	**ARGUMENT** Construct an argument (e.g., detailed outline, poster, or essay) that responds to the compelling question—"How can media be used to influence others?"—using specific claims and relevant evidence from the sources provided and one other source, while acknowledging competing views.
	EXTENSION Using the argument as a foundation, design a questionnaire to disseminate to others and use the data collected to predict how the use and misuse of media may influence politics, society, and war in the next decade.
Taking Informed Action	**UNDERSTAND** Consider how the use and misuse of media may have an impact on ensuring an informed citizenry.
	ASSESS Evaluate how the use and misuse of media may threaten democratic ideals.
	ACT Working with a partner, create an infographic, a 30-second commercial, or a public service announcement to inform your peers or your community about how to identify and evaluate credible media sources.

Overview
Inquiry Description

This inquiry leads students through an investigation of the uses and misuses of media such as leaflets and radio broadcasts during the Korean War, and the uses and misuses of media in contemporary society, politics, and war. By investigating the compelling question of how media can be used to influence others, students attempt to explore the uses and misuses of media through historical and contemporary lenses. The formative performance tasks build on knowledge and skills developed through the inquiry and help students demonstrate the specific ways in which media was used and misused during the Korean War and can be used and misused in contemporary society, politics, and war.

Some knowledge of historical events and ideas is a prerequisite for this inquiry. Thus, students should be somewhat familiar with the impact that media has on influencing others and the phenomenon of "fake news."

This inquiry is expected to take three 40-minute class periods. The inquiry timeframe could expand if teachers think their students need additional instructional experiences (i.e., supporting questions, formative performance tasks, and featured sources). Teachers are encouraged to adapt the inquiries in order to meet the requirements and interests of their particular students. Resources can also be modified as necessary to meet individualized education programs (IEPs) or Section 504 plans for students with disabilities.

Structure of the Inquiry

In addressing the compelling question "Can media be used to influence others?" students work through a series of supporting questions, formative performance tasks, and featured sources in order to construct an argument supported by evidence while acknowledging competing perspectives.

STAGING THE COMPELLING QUESTION
In staging the compelling question, teachers may prompt students with a clip from a U.S. military primary source video depicting the use of communications media (e.g., print leaflets, radio broadcasts) during the Korean War.

SUPPORTING QUESTION 1
The first supporting question—"How was media used and misused during the Korean War?—asks students to view two clips from veterans, and explore primary source artifacts. The formative performance task asks students to demonstrate specific ways in which media was used and misused during the Korean War. Two of the featured sources for this question are video clips from the Korean War Legacy Foundation, and the third source consists of primary source artifacts (leaflets) from the Korean War Legacy Foundation.

Featured Source A is a video clip from a Korean War Legacy Foundation interview with Charles Gaush, in which he discusses the use of media during the Korean War. In Featured Source B, also a video clip from a Korean War Legacy Foundation interview, Norman Renouf discusses media techniques used by the Chinese in the Prisoner of War camps during the war. Featured Source C is a primary source set of artifacts depicting media leaflets used on the battlefield during the war; these artifacts are part of the Korean War Legacy Foundation archives.

SUPPORTING QUESTION 2

The second supporting question asks, "How is media used and misused in contemporary society, politics, and war?" The formative performance task asks students to demonstrate specific ways in which media is used and misused in the contemporary context. Augmenting the previous featured sources, those offered here provide students with additional materials that allow them to explore the uses and misuses of contemporary media in society, politics, and war.

Featured Source A is a short video from Teaching Tolerance about how fake news becomes news. Featured Source B is an interview transcript from VOX addressing how social media is changing conflict in the contemporary world. Featured Source C is a selection of slides from a 2017 presentation on "The New Age of Politics and Media," by Lee Rainie, director of internet and technology research at the Pew Research Center.

SUMMATIVE PERFORMANCE TASK

At this point in the inquiry, students have explored how media was used and misused during the Korean War, and have examined how media is used and misused in contemporary society, politics, and war.

Students should be able to demonstrate the breadth of their understanding and their ability to use evidence from multiple sources to support their claims. In this task, students construct an evidence-based argument using multiple sources to answer the compelling question, "How can media be used to influence others?" Students' arguments may take a variety of forms, including a detailed outline, poster, or essay.

Students' arguments will vary, but could include any of the following:

- During times of war, media can be used and misused as a weapon of war against the enemy.

- Media can be used to influence political decisions.

- Media can be used to promote false or fake news.

To extend students' arguments, teachers may have students design a questionnaire for dissemination to their peers to predict how the use and misuse of media may influence politics and society in the coming decade.

Students have the opportunity to take informed action by drawing on their understandings about ways in which the use and misuse of media may influence politics and society. To understand, students can consider how the use and misuse of media may have an impact on ensuring an informed citizenry. To assess the issue, students will evaluate how the use and misuse of media may threaten democratic ideals. To act, students will create either an infographic, a 30-second commercial, or a public service announcement to inform their peers or others in the community about how to identify and evaluate credible media sources.

Staging the Compelling Question

FEATURED SOURCE Periscope Film, *The Big Picture Psychological Warfare in the Korean War* (35012), archival U.S. military video (from counter 14:00 to 22:43) depicting the use of media during the Korean War.

https://archive.org/details/35012PsychologicalWarfare

SOURCE: PERISCOPE FILM, LLC

Supporting Question 1

FEATURED SOURCE Source A: Oral history interview with Korean War veteran Charles Gaush, in which he discusses the use of media (leaflets) during the Korean War.

https://koreanwarlegacy.org/interviews/charles-gaush

USED WITH PERMISSION FROM THE KOREAN WAR LEGACY PROJECT

Charles Gaush recalls his time in the U.S. Army's psychological warfare unit, and describes creating, designing, photographing, and printing propaganda leaflets in Russian, Korean, and Chinese during the Korean War. He continued to work as a psychological warfare specialist after the Armistice, and describes making leaflets that were dropped in South Korea to give civilians suggestions to improve health and water quality.

Supporting Question 1

FEATURED SOURCE Source B: Oral history interview with Korean War veteran Norman Renouf, in which he discusses the media techniques used by the Chinese in the Prisoner of War camps during the Korean War.

https://koreanwarlegacy.org/interviews/norman-renouf

USED WITH PERMISSION FROM THE KOREAN WAR LEGACY PROJECT

Norman Renouf enlisted in the army at the time of the Korean War and was sent to Korea, where he served as a machine gunner. He was captured by the Chinese in 1951 and was detained in a camp for prisoners of war. He describes the classes that he was forced to take in the camp, which sought to encourage the soldiers to reject capitalism in favor of communist ideology.

Supporting Question 1

FEATURED SOURCE Source C: Korean War Legacy Foundation, primary source set of media artifacts (leaflets) used on the battlefield during the Korean War.

http://www.kwvdm.org/detail_artifact.php?no=2161

The front of a flyer dropped by an airplane encouraging North Koreans to surrender to the United Nations. In the flyer, a North Korean defector describes how he surrendered and states that he chose freedom and is living comfortably in a UN camp.

http://www.kwvdm.org/detail_artifact.php?no=2162

The back of a flyer dropped by an airplane encouraging North Koreans to surrender to the United Nations. The message of the flyer is: "the UN treats us well."

http://www.kwvdm.org/detail_artifact.php?no=2163

The front of a letter written to North Koreans interested in helping the North Korean 45th division to encourage them to defect to the United Nations forces. The letter tells the story of a North Korean security guard who defected to the UN forces.

SAFE CONDUCT PASS
USED WITH PERMISSION FROM THE KOREAN WAR LEGACY PROJECT

Additional images at:

http://www.kwvdm.org/detail_artifact.php?no=42

http://www.kwvdm.org/detail_artifact.php?no=1039

http://www.kwvdm.org/detail_artifact.php?no=1035

http://www.kwvdm.org/detail_artifact.php?no=1040

Supporting Question 2

FEATURED SOURCE Source A: *Teaching Tolerance, video, How* Does Fake News Become News?, 2017.

https://www.youtube.com/watch?v=qcRWkkSvfj0

Supporting Question 2

FEATURED SOURCE Source B: Transcript of a VOX interview with David Patrikarakos, author of *War in 140 Characters* (2017).

https://www.vox.com/world/2017/12/8/16690352/social-media-war-facebook-twitter-russia

"SOCIAL MEDIA HAS TRANSFORMED THE WAY THAT WARS ARE WAGED, COVERED, AND CONSUMED."

David Patrikarakos, a London-based author and journalist, begins his book, *War in 140 Characters*, with this claim. Though wars are still fought on the battlefield, he argues that they are increasingly shaped by competing narratives on social media.

Supporting Question 2

FEATURED SOURCE Source C: Lee Rainie (director of internet and technology research at Pew Research Center), selected slides from a presentation, "The New Age of Politics and Media," Flagler College, St. Augustine, Florida, February 16, 2017.

http://www.pewinternet.org/2017/02/27/the-new-age-of-politics-and-media

THREE DIGITAL TECHNOLOGY REVOLUTIONS IN THE PAST GENERATION

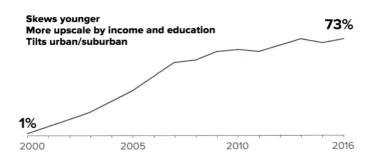

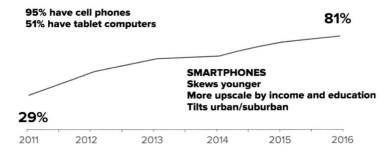

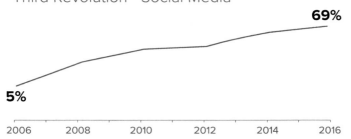

CHAPTER 10

What Does It Mean
to Sacrifice?

Mona Al-Hayani and John Lee

Former prisoners of war in a medical clearing station after their release.

WHAT DOES IT MEAN TO SACRIFICE?	
C3 Framework Indicator	**D2.His.3.6-8.** Use questions generated about individuals and groups to analyze why they, and the developments they shaped, are seen as historically significant. **D2.His.5.6-8.** Explain how and why perspectives of people have changed over time.
Staging the Compelling Question	Discuss the historical significance of individual and group sacrifice in times of conflict and war.

SUPPORTING QUESTION 1	SUPPORTING QUESTION 2
How did soldiers sacrifice during the war?	How did Koreans sacrifice during the war?
FORMATIVE PERFORMANCE TASK	**FORMATIVE PERFORMANCE TASK**
Make a list of examples of the sacrifices of soldiers in the Korean War.	Write a paragraph about the sacrifices of Koreans in the Korean War.
FEATURED SOURCES	**FEATURED SOURCES**
Source A: Chapter from the Korean War Legacy Project, "POW Experience" **Source B:** Personal narrative by Bob Mitchell, a Marine Corps veteran, on his extensive front-line combat experience **Source C:** Personal narrative by Fred Liddell, Korean War veteran, on his capture by Chinese troops in 1951 **Source D:** Link to the Korean War Legacy Project's Memory Bank to search for interviews with other veterans describing soldiers' sacrifices	**Source A:** Chapter from the Korean War Legacy Project, "The Human Experience" **Source B:** Personal narrative of Donald J. Zoeller, 140th Anti-Aircraft Battalion, on his experiences near the main line of resistance (MLR) **Source C:** Personal narrative of Clarence Jerke, 2nd Infantry Division Headquarters Battery, on his work maintaining communications lines behind enemy lines **Source D:** Photograph of Seoul, October 18, 1950 and link to the Korean War Legacy Project's Memory Bank to search for additional photographs of and veteran interviews about the sacrifices made by Koreans and Americans.

Summative Performance Task	**ARGUMENT** "What does it mean to sacrifice?" Construct an argument (e.g., detailed outline, poster, or essay) that discusses the compelling question using specific claims and relevant evidence from the sources provided, as well as one other source, while acknowledging competing views.
	EXTENSION Using the argument as a foundation, engage in small-group brainstorming to create an original poem or song responding to the compelling question, "What does it mean to sacrifice?"
Taking Informed Action	**UNDERSTAND** Examine the historical significance of sacrifices made by individuals and groups during a current or recent conflict or war.
	ASSESS Determine some ways the stories of soldiers fighting abroad might be shared in the community.
	ACT Organize a school- or community-wide effort to share poems or songs of appreciation from students with local veterans' associations.

Overview
Inquiry Description

This inquiry leads students through an investigation of individual and group sacrifices made during times of conflict and war. By investigating the compelling question "What does it mean to sacrifice?" students evaluate the historical significance of individuals and groups during the Korean War. The formative performance tasks build on knowledge and skills through the course of the inquiry and help students to understand the sacrifices made by soldiers and civilians on both sides during the Korean War. Students create an evidence-based argument about the sacrifice of all in times of conflict and war.

Some knowledge of historical events and ideas is a prerequisite for this inquiry. Thus, students should already have a general understanding of the concept of prisoners of war (POWs).

This inquiry is expected to take five 40-minute class periods. The inquiry time frame could expand if teachers think their students need additional instructional experiences (i.e., supporting questions, formative performance tasks, and featured sources). Teachers are encouraged to adapt the inquiries in order to meet the requirements and interests of their particular students. Resources can also be modified as necessary to meet individualized education programs (IEPs) or Section 504 plans for students with disabilities.

Structure of the Inquiry

In addressing the compelling question "What does it mean to sacrifice?" students work through a series of supporting questions, formative performance tasks, and featured sources in order to construct an argument supported by evidence while acknowledging competing perspectives.

STAGING THE COMPELLING QUESTION

In staging the compelling question "What does it mean to sacrifice?" teachers may prompt students with the short documentary, "Beyond the Bridge of No Return: Legacy of a Korean War Veteran." The documentary is available online at https://vimeo.com/hellofuturestories/review/250984755/85a5000301#.

SUPPORTING QUESTION 1

The first supporting question—"How did soldiers sacrifice during the war?"—urges students to think critically about the role of individual and group sacrifice among soldiers during the Korean War. The formative performance task asks students to make a list of examples of the sacrifices of soldiers in the Korean War using two video clips of interviews with veterans about their experiences with sacrifice during the Korean War.

Featured Source A is a chapter, "POW Experience," from the Korean War Legacy Project. Featured Source B is the personal narrative of Bob Mitchell, a Marine Corps veteran who had extensive front-line combat experience in the Korean War. Mitchell recalls the guilt of living through the war while the rest of his friends and comrades died. Featured Source C is the personal narrative of Fred Liddell, who was captured in 1951 by Chinese troops. Liddell provides an account of his capture and the details surrounding it, including the policy of "lenient treatment." Further research about this policy would be a valuable learning exercise for students, as it offers insight into propaganda techniques used on POWs. Students might also search the Korean War Legacy Project Memory Bank to locate other veteran interviews describing the sacrifices made by soldiers.

SUPPORTING QUESTION 2

The second supporting question—"How did Koreans sacrifice during the war?"—asks students to think about the ways Koreans sacrificed during the war. The formative performance task asks students to write a paragraph about the sacrifices of Koreans in the Korean War.

Featured Source A is a chapter, "The Human Experience," from the Korean War Legacy Project. It is available at https://koreanwarlegacy.org/chapters/the-human-experience/.

Featured Source B is the personal narrative of Donald Zoeller, member of the 140th Anti-Aircraft Battalion near the main line of resistance (MLR). Zoeller reflects on helping an orphaned Korean boy. The clip, full interview, and transcript are available at https://koreanwarlegacy.org/interviews/donald-j-zoeller-2/.

Featured Source C is the personal narrative of Clarence Jerke, member of the 2nd Infantry Division Headquarters Battery, who worked behind enemy lines maintaining communications. In his interview, Jerke describes how starving civilians would jump on the back of his truck as it was moving and throw food out to their friends. The clip, full interview, and transcript are available at https://koreanwarlegacy.org/interviews/clarence-jerke/.

Featured Source D is a photograph of a residential neighborhood in Seoul that was largely destroyed by the Korean War. The capitol building can be seen in the background. Students are encouraged to use the link provided to search the Korean War Legacy Project Memory Bank to locate more photographs and other veteran interviews describing the sacrifices made by Koreans during the war.

These sources provide students with primary and secondary sources of data about the sacrifices made by Koreans during the war. After students examine the sources, they will write a paragraph about the sacrifices of Koreans during the Korean War.

SUMMATIVE PERFORMANCE TASK

At this point in the inquiry, students have examined the sacrifices of U.S. and Korean soldiers and Korean civilians on both sides of the war.

Students should be able to demonstrate the breadth of their understanding and their ability to use evidence from multiple sources to support their claims. In this task, students construct an evidence-based argument using multiple sources to answer the compelling question "What does it mean to sacrifice?" Students' arguments will take a variety of forms, including a detailed outline, poster, or essay.

Students' arguments will vary, but could include either of the following:

- Sacrifice means putting the needs of others before yourself.

- Sacrifice means fighting for the freedom and democracy of others.

To extend students' arguments, teachers may have them engage in small-group brainstorming sessions to create an original poem or song responding to the compelling question "What does it mean to sacrifice?"

Students have the opportunity to take informed action by drawing on their understandings of individual and group sacrifices during times of conflict and war. To *understand*, students can examine the historical significance of sacrifices made by individuals and groups during times of conflict and war. To *assess* the issue, students can determine some ways the stories of soldiers fighting abroad might be shared with the local community. To *act*, students can organize a school- or community-wide effort to share poems or songs of appreciation from students with local veterans' associations.

Staging the Compelling Question

FEATURED SOURCE Source: Documentary short, *The Legacy: A Documentary from the Korean War Legacy Project.*

https://vimeo.com/hellofuturestories/review/250984755/85a5000301#

IMAGE USED WITH PERMISSION FROM THE KOREAN WAR LEGACY PROJECT

Supporting Question 1

FEATURED SOURCE Source A: A chapter from "POW Experience" by the Korean War Legacy Project.

http://koreanwarlegacy.org/chapters/the-pow-experience

IMAGE USED WITH PERMISSION FROM THE KOREAN WAR LEGACY PROJECT

Supporting Question 1

FEATURED SOURCE Source B: Personal narrative by Bob Mitchell discussing his experience with survivor guilt.

https://koreanwarlegacy.org/interviews/bob-mitchell

USED WITH PERMISSION FROM THE KOREAN WAR LEGACY PROJECT

Bob Mitchell is a Marine Corps veteran with extensive front-line combat experience in the Korean War. In this video clip, Mitchell recalls with great emotion the survivor guilt he experienced after surviving the war while the rest of his company was overwhelmed and killed by the Chinese. Mitchell says he eventually reached the realization that such experiences are simply the reality of war—some people make it and others don't.

Supporting Question 1

FEATURED SOURCE Source C: Personal narrative by Fred Liddell discussing his experience of being captured by Chinese troops in 1951.

https://koreanwarlegacy.org/interviews/fred-liddell

IMAGE CREDIT: JONGWOO HAN. USED WITH PERMISSION FROM THE KOREAN WAR LEGACY PROJECT

In this video clip, Fred Liddell vividly discusses his 1951 capture by Chinese troops. He provides a detailed, articulate account of his capture and the details surrounding it. He also mentions the policy of "lenient treatment" in this clip.

Supporting Question 1

Source D: Link to the Korean War Legacy Project's Memory Bank, to search for other veteran interviews describing soldiers' sacrifices.

https://koreanwarlegacy.org/interactive-library

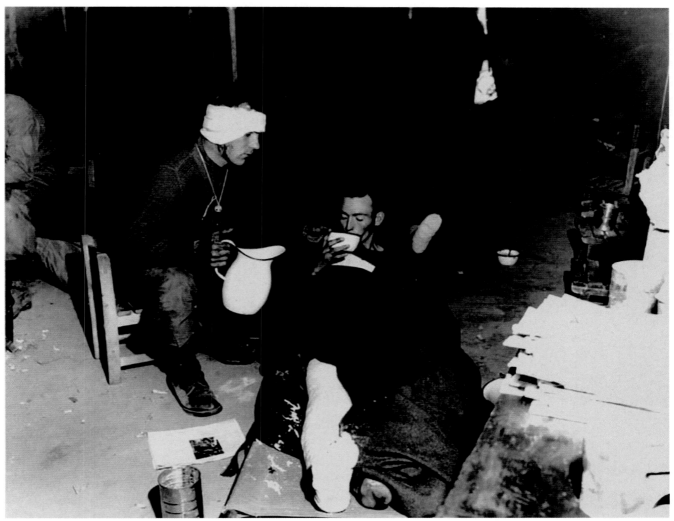

USED WITH PERMISSION FROM THE KOREAN WAR LEGACY PROJECT

Wounded soldiers at a Mobile Army Surgical Hospital.

Supporting Question 2

FEATURED SOURCE Source A: A chapter from "The Human Experience" by the Korean War Legacy Project.

https://koreanwarlegacy.org/chapters/the-human-experience

USED WITH PERMISSION FROM THE KOREAN WAR LEGACY PROJECT

Supporting Question 2

FEATURED SOURCE Source B: Personal narrative by Donald J. Zoeller, discussing his experience helping an orphaned Korean boy.

https://koreanwarlegacy.org/interviews/donald-j-zoeller-2

USED WITH PERMISSION FROM THE KOREAN WAR LEGACY PROJECT

Donald J. Zoeller was a member of the 140th Anti-Aircraft Battalion near the main line of resistance (MLR) in the Korean War. In this video clip, Zoeller says that he did not get to know many Korean people, as he was always outside of the cities. However, he goes on to detail an exceptional experience in which he met a young Korean boy who was orphaned. Zoeller invited the boy to stay with the soldiers, and later brought him safely to an orphanage.

Supporting Question 2

FEATURED SOURCE Source C: Personal narrative by Clarence Jerke detailing his work maintaining communications lines behind enemy lines during the Korean War.

https://koreanwarlegacy.org/interviews/clarence-jerke

USED WITH PERMISSION FROM THE KOREAN WAR LEGACY PROJECT

Clarence Jerke, a member of the 2nd Infantry Division Headquarters Battery, worked behind enemy lines maintaining communications lines during the Korean War. In this interview, Jerke describes seeing starving civilians jump onto his truck while it was moving and attempt to steal food by throwing it over the sides of the truck to their friends.

Supporting Question 2

FEATURED SOURCE Source D: Photograph of destruction in Seoul, October 18, 1950. The Korean War Legacy Project's searchable Memory Bank includes additional images and veteran interviews related to this inquiry.

https://koreanwarlegacy.org/interactive-library

USED WITH PERMISSION FROM THE KOREAN WAR LEGACY PROJECT

CHAPTER 11

Can **Words** Lead to War?

Mona Al-Hayani and John Lee

Kim Jong-un and Donald Trump, June 2018.

CAN WORDS LEAD TO WAR?

C3 Framework Indicator	**D2.His.4.6-8**. Analyze multiple factors that influenced the perspectives of people during different historical eras.
Staging the Compelling Question	Discuss the impact of words within particular historical eras while viewing a video clip from Al Jazeera: "Trump Escalates Threats on North Korea as Tensions Rise."

SUPPORTING QUESTION 1	SUPPORTING QUESTION 2	SUPPORTING QUESTION 3
How do world leaders use the media to communicate their messages?	How have contemporary American presidents communicated with North Korea?	What historical events from the Korean Conflict might escalate current diplomatic tensions?
FORMATIVE PERFORMANCE TASK	**FORMATIVE PERFORMANCE TASK**	**FORMATIVE PERFORMANCE TASK**
Make a timeline of the historical evolution of media used by world leaders to communicate their messages.	Make a Venn diagram illustrating how presidents Clinton, Bush, Obama, and Trump have communicated with North Korea.	Create an infographic describing U.S. diplomatic tensions with North Korea during the Clinton, Bush, Obama, and Trump administrations.
FEATURED SOURCES	**FEATURED SOURCES**	**FEATURED SOURCES**
Source A: Article, "8 Presidential Communication Firsts," Nick Keppler, MentalFloss.com **Source B:** Article, "How Presidents Communicate with the Public Will Surprise You," K. C. Morgan, RealClear Politics	**Source A:** Article, "How Trump's Predecessors Dealt with the North Korean Threat," Russell Goldman, *The New York Times* **Source B:** Article, "Trump's Year of Taunting, Teasing and Threatening Kim Jong-un," Julie Vitkovskaya, *The Washington Post*	**Source A:** Article, "Trump's North Korea Tweets Renew Debate over Nuclear Authority," Ashleigh Killough, CNN **Source B:** Article, "The U.S. and North Korea on the Brink: A Timeline," Priyanka Boghani, PBS Frontline **Source C:** Speech, Kim Jong-un responding to a UN address by Donald Trump, National Committee on North Korea Database

Summative Performance Task	**ARGUMENT** "Can words lead to war?" Construct an argument (e.g., an essay, outline, or poster) that responds to the compelling question using specific claims and relevant evidence from the sources provided, as well as one other source, while acknowledging competing views.
	EXTENSION Using the argument as a foundation, engage in an informed debate or Socratic Seminar responding to the compelling question.
Taking Informed Action	**UNDERSTAND** Examine the role social media plays in international diplomacy.
	ASSESS Consider whether social media should be used as a communication platform for world leaders.
	ACT Compose an op-ed letter or article for your school or local newspaper, using specific claims and relevant evidence, discussing the impact social media has on contemporary diplomatic tensions.

Overview
Inquiry Description

This inquiry leads students through an investigation of the importance words have in easing or escalating diplomatic tensions. By investigating the compelling question "Can words lead to war?" students evaluate the historical context of American tensions with North Korea. The formative performance tasks build on knowledge and skills through the course of the inquiry and help students trace the evolution of the contemporary Korean conflict through an analysis of how contemporary American presidents have communicated in general and specifically with North Korea. Students create an evidence-based argument about whether words can lead to war, and about the implications of social media for international diplomacy.

Some knowledge of historical events and ideas is a prerequisite for this inquiry. Thus, students should have already studied or be somewhat familiar with contemporary tensions between the United States and North Korea.

This inquiry is expected to take three to four 40-minute class periods. The inquiry time frame could expand if teachers think that their students need additional instructional experiences (i.e., supporting questions, formative performance tasks, and featured sources). Teachers are encouraged to adapt the inquiries to meet the requirements and interests of their students. Resources can also be modified as necessary to meet individualized education programs (IEPs) or Section 504 plans for students with disabilities.

Structure of the Inquiry

In addressing the compelling question "Can words lead to war?" students work through a series of supporting questions, formative performance tasks, and featured sources in order to construct an argument supported by evidence while acknowledging competing perspectives.

STAGING THE COMPELLING QUESTION

In staging the compelling question, "Can words lead to war?" teachers may prompt a discussion among students about the impact of words within particular historical eras with a video clip from Al Jazeera, "Trump Escalates Threats on North Korea as Tensions Rise." The discussion can provide an opportunity for students to express their opinions and to organize their existing knowledge about how the words of world leaders convey messages that may be viewed by others as threats and may lead to increased tensions.

SUPPORTING QUESTION 1

The first supporting question—"How do world leaders use the media to communicate their messages?"—has students thinking critically about the role media plays in governmental communications.

The formative performance task asks students to read two articles: Featured Source A, "8 Presidential Communication Firsts," from Mental Floss, and Featured Source B, "How Presidents Communicate with the Public Will Surprise You," by K. C. Morgan at RealClear Politics. These sources provide students with a historical overview of presidential communication in terms of both the technologies used and the styles of individual leaders. After students have read the articles, the formative performance task asks them to make a timeline of the historical evolution of media used by American presidents to communicate their messages.

SUPPORTING QUESTION 2

The second supporting question—"How have contemporary American presidents communicated with North Korea?"—has students compare and contrast the ways in which U.S. presidents have communicated with North Korea in the contemporary era.

In preparation for the formative performance task for this question, students will read two additional articles. Featured Source A is a *New York Times* article by Russell Goldman, "How Trump's Predecessors Dealt with the North Korean Threat." Featured Source B is a *Washington Post* article by Julie Vitkovskaya, "Trump's Year of Taunting, Teasing and Threatening Kim Jong Un." After students read the articles, they will make a Venn diagram comparing how presidents Clinton, Bush, Obama, and Trump have communicated with North Korea and will discuss how these communications may exacerbate diplomatic tensions.

SUPPORTING QUESTION 3

The third supporting question—"What historical events from the Korean conflict might escalate current diplomatic tensions?"—encourages students to explore historical events during the Korean conflict and analyze the role these events may have played in escalating current diplomatic tensions between the United States and North Korea.

Featured Source A is an article by Ashleigh Killough on the CNN website, "Trump's North Korea Tweets Renew Debate over Nuclear Authority." Featured Source B is an article by Priyanka Boghani, from PBS Frontline, "The U.S. and North Korea on the Brink: A Timeline." Featured Source C is the text of North Korean leader Kim Jong-un's speech made on September 22, 2017 in response to President Trump's comments to the United Nations General Assembly just three days earlier—which teachers might also want students to read or watch.

For this question's formative performance task, students will create an infographic describing U.S. diplomatic tensions with North Korea during the Clinton, Bush, Obama, and Trump administrations.

SUMMATIVE PERFORMANCE TASK

At this point in the inquiry, students have examined how world leaders can use the media to communicate their messages, how historical events during the Korean conflict have the potential for escalating current diplomatic tensions, and how contemporary American presidents (Clinton, Bush, Obama, and Trump) have communicated with North Korea.

Students should be able to demonstrate the breadth of their understanding and their ability to use evidence from multiple sources to support their claims. In this task, students construct an evidence-based argument using multiple sources to answer the compelling question "Can words lead to war?" Students' arguments could take a variety of forms, including a detailed outline, poster, or essay.

Students' arguments will vary, but could include any of the following:

- Words lead to war because international leaders may use media outlets to spread propaganda.

- Words lead to war by creating tension and conflict among nations.

- Words cannot lead to war because modern countries know wars are too costly if they are based only on words.

To extend their arguments, teachers may have students engage in an informed debate or Socratic Seminar analyzing the compelling question "Can words lead to war?"

Students have the opportunity to take informed action by drawing on their understanding of the current and historical relationship between the United States and North Korea. To understand, students can examine the impact that social media now has on international diplomacy. To assess the issue, students can consider whether social media should be used as a communication platform for world leaders. To act, students can compose an op-ed letter or article for their school or local newspaper, using specific claims and relevant evidence, discussing the impact of social media on diplomatic tensions.

Staging the Compelling Question

FEATURED SOURCE Source: Article, "Trump Escalates Threats on North Korea as Tensions Rise" (excerpt).

http://www.aljazeera.com/news/2017/08/trump-escalates-threats-north-korea-tension-rise-170810223728805.html

Doubling down on his war of words, U.S. President Donald Trump warned Kim Jong-un's government on Thursday to "get their act together" or face extraordinary "trouble," and suggested his earlier threat to unleash "fire and fury" on North Korea was too mild.

"Maybe that statement wasn't tough enough," Trump said, in the latest U.S. salvo in an escalating exchange of threats between the nuclear-armed nations.

A day after North Korea laid out plans to strike near Guam with unsettling specificity, there was no observable march toward combat, despite the angry rhetoric from both sides. U.S. officials said there was no major movement of U.S. military assets to the region, nor were there signs Pyongyang was actively preparing for war.

Supporting Question 1

FEATURED SOURCE Source A: Nick Keppler, "8 Presidential Communication Firsts," MentalFloss. com, March 13, 2016.

http://mentalfloss.com/article/77071/8-presidential-communication-firsts

When Franklin Roosevelt declared "I want to talk for a few minutes with the people of the United States about banking" in a radio address to the American people on March 12, 1933, he was making history. The address—in which Roosevelt explained his reasoning behind calling a banking holiday to reorganize the battered industry and to announce its reopening—was the first of FDR's "fireside chats," which represented a game-changing communications strategy and use of technology for the White House. Roosevelt bypassed the news media and spoke directly to the citizenry, creating an aura of calmness and confidence during the Great Depression and World War II (though he never gave a radio address near an actual fireplace). Here are eight other firsts and breakthroughs in presidential communication.

1. First State of the Union Address / George Washington

Article II, Section 3 of the Constitution stipulates that the president "shall from time to time give to Congress information of the State of the Union and recommend to their Consideration such measures as he shall judge necessary and expedient." The task first fell to George Washington eight months after his inauguration. On January 8, 1790, the former general addressed Congress at the provincial capital of New York City. Because the nation was new, the address covered some basics of maintaining a country. Washington called for the creation of a standing army; money to fund foreign relations; a process for naturalizing foreigners, "[u]niformity in the currency, weights, and measures," and "the promotion of science and literature."

2. First Telegraph Line / Abraham Lincoln

Congress authorized funding for Samuel F. B. Morse to build a test telegraph between Washington, DC and Baltimore in 1843. While Lincoln's may not have been the first administration to send or receive information via telegraph, it was the first to have a line installed in the War Department, starting in May 1862. (Previously, public officials who wanted to wire a message had to stand in line in a clerk's office with everyone else.) Throughout the Civil War, Lincoln used the line extensively, starting his day by shifting through communications from various state governors and generals. Some nights, he even slept in the telegraph room. The wire also allowed him to directly oversee the war, giving specific orders for movements and troop counts.

3. First Telephone Line / Rutherford B. Hayes

Fred A. Gower, the managing agent of Alexander Graham Bell, personally oversaw the installation of the first telephone line in the White House in 1877. Gower helped President Rutherford B. Hayes dial up Bell at a hotel in Providence, Rhode Island, in June of that year. According to the *Providence Journal*, "The President listened carefully while a gradually increasing smile wreathed his lips, and wonder shone in his eyes more and more, until he took the little instrument from his ear, looked at it a moment in surprise, and remarked, 'That is wonderful.'" The phone was connected permanently to the only other one in Washington, that of the Treasury Department.

4. First Radio Address / Warren G. Harding

Roosevelt was not the first president heard over the airwaves. That honor goes to Warren G. Harding. On June 14, 1922, Harding gave a speech to commemorate the unveiling of a memorial to Francis Scott Key. Due to concerns that too many people would want to hear Harding speak for the venue to accommodate, the decision was made to broadcast the speech on radio. Originally, a transmitting station was going to be built in Baltimore, but that was deemed too expensive. Instead, Harding's voice was transmitted via telephone to the Anacostia broadcasting station and then broadcast from Anacostia to the people of Baltimore. A few months later, Harding used the same transmit-to-Anacostia trick for his State of the Union, which, according to a contemporary *New York Times* article, was "passed along through relay stations to a good part of the country," including his sick wife.

5. First Televised Address / Harry Truman

There were 44,000 TVs in the United States when President Harry Truman made the first televised primetime address on October 5, 1947. Truman essentially called on Americans to eat less, saving the country's excess food supply for European countries still recovering from World War II. Truman suggested Americans skip meat on Tuesdays and eggs and poultry on Thursdays and set aside a slice of bread each day. He also suggested restaurants skip the complimentary bread and butter. "We believe that self-control is the best control," he said. "From now on, we shall be testing at every meal the degree to which each of us is willing to exercise self-control for the good of all."

6. First Email / Bill Clinton

Bill Clinton has often said that the first email he sent as president was to astronaut John Glenn, who had recently boarded the International Space Station to test the effects of space on aging. But as *The Atlantic* confirmed last year, this is a complete myth. John Gibbons, Clinton's Science Advisor, explained, "we wanted to introduce the President to email and the Net. So we brought him over to the old EOB [Executive Office Building], and he sat down in front of this computer—it may have been the first time he sat down in front of a computer—and we showed him how email worked and gave him his email address over across the street in the Oval Office. So he typed in his first email message. It was something like, 'Bill Clinton, it's time to come home for lunch. Signed, Hillary,' something like that. I saved a copy of it. That was his first email." And in 1994, the New York Times reported on an email that Clinton sent to the Prime Minister of Sweden. And in what was described as a breach of netiquette even back then, it was "COMPOSED ENTIRELY OF CAPITAL LETTERS."

7. First Webchat / Bill Clinton

Almost exactly a year after his purported exchange with Glenn, Clinton became the first president to take questions from Internet users in a forum hosted by the Democratic Leadership Council and the Internet company Excite@Home. Digital communications had boomed during his administration. In 1993, 1.3 million computers were connected to the web. By 1999, 56 million were online. For 90 minutes on November 8, 1999, a moderator sorted through questions posed to Clinton and an assistant typed out his answers. (The 53-year-old president admitted to being "technologically challenged.") About 50,000 watched the video feed. Clinton responded to a questioner that the chances of a peace agreement between Israelis and Palestinians were "better than 50-50." He also told "Cynthia in Arizona" that he was not hoarding food in preparation for the Y2K [Year 2000] computer crash.

8. First Tweet / Barack Obama

Barack Obama's 2008 presidential campaign made unprecedented use of social media. When he was elected to office, his staff instituted the White House Twitter account, while political allies kept up his @BarackObama. Obama never sent a tweet from his own fingers, however, until a tour of the Red Cross's Washington, D.C. headquarters on January 18, 2010. A Red Cross employee apparently coaxed Obama to hit the "send" button on a tweet reading, "President Obama and the First Lady are here visiting our disaster operation center right now," marking the first tweet physically delivered by a U.S. president. On May 18, 2015, Obama established his own Twitter account, @POTUS.

USED WITH PERMISSION FROM MENTAL FLOSS

Supporting Question 1

FEATURED SOURCE Source B: K. C. Morgan, "How Presidents Communicate with the Public Will Surprise You," RealClear Politics, January 15, 2016.

http://www.realclear.com/history/2016/01/15/how_presidents_communicate_with_the_public_will_surprise_you_12694.html

HOW PRESIDENTS COMMUNICATE WITH THE PUBLIC WILL SURPRISE YOU

For the most recent State of the Union address, President Barack Obama appeared on primetime TV on just about every channel. But it wasn't always this way. Once upon a time, the President of the United States used all sorts of ways to talk to the American people.

FDR's Weekly Address

President Franklin D. Roosevelt reached out to the American people once a week by radio while he was in office and his fireside chats are the stuff of legend, but he wasn't the first to do so. FDR just addressed the nation so often, he became famous for it.

Reagan Does the Radio

President Ronald Reagan brought back Roosevelt's weekly radio broadcasts while he served the nation. Later presidents modernized the practice while maintaining it. George W. Bush did his by podcast. Barack Obama does short videos for the Internet.

Coolidge Makes History

It was President Calvin Coolidge who first addressed the American public live from a national platform: the radio. His 1923 State of the Union speech was broadcast nationwide.

Truman on TV

The first president to deliver a televised address was Harry Truman. He addressed the nation in 1947 from the White House to ask the public to use less grain. This was to help those starving in Europe, riddled with famine after World War II. Only a few thousand people in the country had television sets at this time.

George Washington's State of the Union

Appropriately, George Washington was the first president to deliver a State of the Union address. He helped to make the speech a yearly thing after he spoke at Federal Hall in New York City in January, 1790. He praised the first-ever session of Congress and outlined his plan for the coming year. His goals involved building roads for the postal service, creating a uniform measuring system for the new country, and shoring up the army.

Johnson in Primetime

Though Truman was the first to televise his State of the Union, it was LBJ who turned it into must-watch TV. He went on primetime in 1965 to give his address. President Johnson spoke about civil rights reform and wanted to appear at night in order to reach a larger audience.

Clinton [Takes It] Online

Bill Clinton was the first president to take his State of the Union worldwide. His 1997 address to America was the first to be broadcast live on the Internet.

Washington Says Farewell

Before radio, before television, way before the Internet, presidents didn't get to talk to the whole nation all at once. In 1796, George Washington delivered his Farewell Address by letter. It was published in newspapers across the new nation, and was even printed up in pamphlet form for distribution.

The Gettysburg Address

Heralded as one of the greatest of all presidential speeches—truly the president of all speeches—the Gettysburg Address was delivered mainly to an audience of military personnel, politicians, reporters, and some spectators. There was little applause following President Lincoln's famous words, which were reprinted in newspapers all over the United States and skewered by some media outlets.

USED WITH PERMISSION FROM REALCLEAR

Supporting Question 2

FEATURED SOURCE   Source A: Russell Goldman, "How Trump's Predecessors Dealt with the North Korean Threat," *The New York Times* (excerpt), August 17, 2017.

https://www.nytimes.com/2017/08/17/world/asia/trump-north-korea-threat.html

HONG KONG — Carrots or sticks? Aid or sanctions? Engagement or containment? American attempts to counter North Korea's nuclear program did not begin last week when President Trump promised to unleash "fire and fury" against the isolated government. For decades, Mr. Trump's predecessors have waded into the diplomatic mire, trying to threaten or cajole North Korea's ruling family into abandoning the country's weapons programs. Each failed.

Supporting Question 2

FEATURED SOURCE   Source B: Julie Vitkovskaya, "Trump's Year of Taunting, Teasing and Threatening Kim Jong Un," *The Washington Post* (excerpt), January 4, 2018.

https://www.washingtonpost.com/news/worldviews/wp/2018/01/04/trumps-year-of-taunting-teasing-and-threatening-kim-jong-un

Relations between the United States and North Korea got off to a rocky start this year. After fireworks lit up the night sky in Pyongyang, North Korean leader Kim Jong Un announced in a televised speech that the United States is within a "nuclear striking range" and the regime's nuclear forces are "a reality."

Supporting Question 3

FEATURED SOURCE Source A: Ashleigh Killough, "Trump's North Korea Tweets Renew Debate over Nuclear Authority," CNN.com (excerpt).

https://www.cnn.com/2018/01/03/politics/trump-nuclear-authority/index.html

Washington (CNN) — President Donald Trump's escalated statements against North Korea have revived questions in Washington about the president's authority to approve the use of nuclear weapons.

Supporting Question 3

FEATURED SOURCE Source B: Priyanka Boghani, "The U.S. and North Korea on the Brink: A Timeline," PBS Frontline, June 12, 2018.

THE U.S. AND NORTH KOREA ON THE BRINK: A TIMELINE

Last year, a war of words between President Donald Trump and Kim Jong-un sparked fears that the escalating rhetoric could spill over into military confrontation. This year, the two appeared to move towards what would be the first-ever meeting between a sitting U.S. president and North Korean leader.

Threats, talks, sanctions, and missile tests are not new developments in the US-North Korea relationship. What's different now, experts say, is that the gap in knowledge about what the other side is thinking seems wider than ever, with North Korean officials puzzling over President Trump's threats, and Americans trying to understand Kim Jong-un's motivations.

Here, we examine the turbulent history between the two countries, from North Korea's work to develop nuclear and missile programs, to U.S. efforts to stop them.

Early Ambitions

North Korea's quest for a nuclear weapon can be traced back decades to the Korean War.

"They felt that they needed to develop a capability that would deter an American attack," said Duyeon Kim, a visiting senior fellow at the Seoul-based Korean Peninsula Future Forum.

The fear was not unfounded. In 1950, President Harry Truman said there was "active consideration" of using the atomic bomb in the conflict. "Ever since the Korean War, they always assumed that Washington would attack them any day and wipe them out," Kim said. "The only way for them to survive and not get attacked would be to develop the most powerful weapon on Earth, which would be the nuclear bomb."

With the help of the Soviet Union, North Korea began work on a nuclear complex, and in the early 1980s, built its first power plant, Yongbyon.

In these early days, Pyongyang insisted that its aims were peaceful. It became party to the Nuclear Nonproliferation Treaty (NPT) in 1985, and signed an agreement in 1991 with its rival South Korea in which both countries agreed not to produce or use nuclear weapons. But as the International Atomic Energy Agency (IAEA) pressed for access to the North's nuclear waste sites, the country warned that it would withdraw from the NPT.

1994-2001: Clinton Tries for a Deal

In early 1994, North Korea threatened to reprocess fuel rods from its nuclear reactor, a step that would give it enough weapons-grade plutonium for five or six nuclear weapons. The Clinton administration considered various responses, including a strike on the Yongbyon facility, but eventually chose to negotiate with Pyongyang. Amid the crisis, Kim Il-sung—the founding dictator of North Korea, who ruled for more than four decades—died. His son, Kim Jong-il, took over as leader.

By October 1994, negotiations resulted in a deal known as the Agreed Framework. Under the framework, North Korea agreed to freeze and eventually dismantle its nuclear facilities, in exchange for a move toward normalizing relations with the United States. North Korea would also receive shipments of fuel oil and assistance with constructing light-water reactor power plants (which would have safeguards to ensure that fuel could not be diverted to weapons).

"The North Koreans agreed to the deal because there was a shift in the geopolitical situation in the late 1980s, early 1990s," said Joel Wit, a senior fellow at the US-Korea Institute at the Johns Hopkins School of Advanced International Studies and one of the negotiators of the Agreed Framework.

"First of all, they lost the Soviet Union as their main ally, and secondly, the Chinese were shifting towards establishing better relations with South Korea," Wit said. "And so the North Koreans made a strategic decision that if they could secure better relations with the United States, they were willing to pay the price. And the price was, of course, their nuclear program."

North Korea shut down its nuclear reactor, and stalled construction of two others. In 1998, it test-fired an intermediate-range missile—the Taepo Dong-1, with an estimated range of 900 to 1,800 miles—that failed. Nevertheless, negotiations kept on. North Korea agreed to a moratorium on testing medium- and long-range missiles as long as talks with the United States continued.

Madeleine Albright, then the secretary of state, visited North Korea's capital in 2000 and met Kim Jong-il. The North Koreans hoped Clinton would also visit before he left office, moving North Korea and the United States closer to normalizing relations. But time ran out with the end of the Clinton presidency.

2001-2003: The Framework Collapses

When President George W. Bush took office in 2001, his administration took a more hardline approach to North Korea, postponing talks and expressing skepticism about whether Pyongyang was adhering to the Agreed Framework. North Korea warned Washington that such tough talk would force it to "strongly react."

Bush listed North Korea among one of three nations in an "axis of evil" in his 2002 State of the Union address. Later that year, in October, the administration said that North Korea was secretly enriching uranium—a claim Pyongyang denied. A month later, the fuel-oil shipments agreed to under President Clinton were suspended. By the end of 2002, North Korea ordered IAEA inspectors out of the country. The Agreed Framework had collapsed.

Experts have described this period as a missed opportunity. Had North Korea not begun enriching uranium, they say, and had the United States moved faster to implement its portion of the agreed framework—including the construction of light-water reactors—things may have gone differently. The Bush administration, said Wit, "thought they could bully the North Koreans into stopping cheating."

By January 2003, the relationship hit a new low with North Korea's official withdrawal from the Nonproliferation Treaty. Four months later, U.S. officials said North Korea admitted to having at least one nuclear weapon.

2003-2006: Six Party Talks Begin

The Bush administration would re-engage with North Korea later in 2003, joining South Korea, Japan, Russia, and China in what came to be known as the Six Party Talks.

The talks produced a joint statement in 2005 in which North Korea once again agreed in principle to give up its nuclear weapons program, rejoin the Nonproliferation Treaty, and accept IAEA inspections, while maintaining that it had the right to peaceful nuclear energy.

In exchange, the five other countries agreed to energy assistance and to discuss giving North Korea light-water reactors "at an appropriate time." The United States and South Korea said they would not deploy nuclear weapons on the Korean Peninsula, and the United States and Japan said they would move toward normalizing relations.

However, progress was short lived. In July 2006, North Korea—angered by U.S. targeting of its financial assets and the pace of the light-water reactor project—broke its 1999 moratorium on testing medium- and long-range missiles. It launched seven ballistic missiles, including the long-range Taepo Dong-2, which if perfected, would have the ability to hit Alaska. The missile failed.

"Under Kim Jong-il's rule, a useful way of understanding the dynamics of North Korea and the United States is the idea of cycles," says Jung H. Pak, a senior fellow at the Brookings Institution's Center for East Asia Policy Studies. "North Korea comes to dialogue, then retracts, using the United States' 'hostile policy' as an excuse to conduct missile or nuclear tests, then re-enters dialogue to dampen sanctions implementation or reduce tension."

2006: A First Nuclear Test

In October 2006, the situation reached a dangerous new stage with North Korea's first nuclear test. The explosion yielded less than a kiloton, per the Nuclear Threat Initiative. For comparison, the atomic bomb that devastated Hiroshima was 15 kilotons.

The United Nations responded swiftly with a resolution requiring North Korea to stop testing nuclear weapons and to abandon its missile program. In response, a representative for the regime said the nuclear test was "entirely attributable to [the] United States' threats, sanctions, and pressure." [The representative] accused the Bush administration of responding to North Korea's "patient and sincere efforts with sanctions and blockades."

The regime's rhetoric aside, the Six Party Talks began to show dividends. In July 2007, North Korea shut down its nuclear facilities at Yongbyon, a move confirmed by a visiting IAEA team. It also agreed to disable the facilities, which would make it harder to restart them. In return, it would receive fuel oil and be removed from the United States' list of state sponsors of terrorism. However, disagreements on how to verify North Korea's actions once again led to a stalemate.

2009: A Second Nuclear Test

President Barack Obama began his first term with an inaugural address telling "leaders around the globe who seek to sow conflict" that "we will extend a hand if you are willing to unclench your fist."

Just three months later, North Korea launched a Unha-2 rocket with the goal of putting a satellite in space. The United States and its allies had warned Pyongyang they would consider the launch a violation of UN resolutions.

The launch failed, and the Security Council again tightened sanctions. Pyongyang, in turn, said it would no longer adhere to any agreements from the Six Party Talks and threatened to reactivate its nuclear facilities. Days later, it ordered IAEA inspectors out of the country.

Then, on May 24, North Korea conducted its second underground nuclear test, estimated to measure four kilotons, according to the Nuclear Threat Initiative. In a statement, it said the test helped "settle the scientific and technological problems" in increasing the power of its nuclear weapons.

Again, sanctions followed—first from the UN Security Council and then [from] the United States. By the fall of 2011, Pyongyang hinted that it would be willing to resume multilateral talks, but then suddenly, North Korean leader Kim Jong-il died in December, after holding power for 17 years. His youngest son, Kim Jong-un, was named North Korea's leader.

2012-2016: Testing Accelerates

The pace of ballistic missile tests and nuclear tests would significantly escalate under Kim Jong-un.

Despite agreeing to a moratorium on nuclear and long-range missile tests with the Obama administration in February 2012, North Korea once again attempted a space launch with the Unha-3 that April. But the test was a failure—the rocket disintegrated shortly after launch. The United States halted food aid in response.

In December 2012, North Korea tried again, this time successfully launching the Unha-3 rocket and putting an object into orbit for the first time in [the country's] history. It maintained that the launch was for peaceful purposes. The rocket was similar in design to a missile that could possibly carry a warhead as far as California. The UN Security Council passed a new resolution a month later, condemning the launch and expanding travel bans and asset freezes for certain individuals and organizations.

The international response would do little to slow the new leader's nuclear ambitions. Between 2013 and 2016, North Korea held three more nuclear tests, each more powerful than the last. In September 2016, North Korea claimed to test its first hydrogen bomb, a claim that experts greeted with skepticism. It also continued to make strides in its ballistic missile program.

North Korea used the nuclear and missile tests to establish "strategic relevance in the region," according to Pak. "We can't underestimate how North Korea was devastated during the Korean War, so the Kim family's goal is to ensure the country's survival, but also their own survival." The missile program, she noted, was "for all of those things—deterring the United States, deterring South Korea, deterring Japan."

2017: A War of Words with Trump

In 2017, North Korea reached two significant milestones. It successfully test-fired its first intercontinental ballistic missiles [ISBMs] in July, capable of reaching Alaska. It once again claimed to successfully test a hydrogen bomb. Whether it was indeed a hydrogen bomb has not been confirmed, but its nuclear test in September was recorded as North Korea's most powerful yet, at an estimated 250 kilotons.

When he addressed the UN General Assembly in September, Trump said that if the United States was forced to defend itself or its allies, it would have "no choice but to totally destroy North Korea." Referring to Kim Jong-un as "Rocket Man," Trump said the North Korean leader was "on a suicide mission for himself and for his regime."

Kim Jong-un responded to Trump's speech by calling the U.S. president "mentally deranged" and warning that he would "pay dearly" for threatening to destroy North Korea. He also said that Trump's comments "have convinced me, rather than frightening or stopping me, that the path I chose is correct and that it is the one I have to follow to the last."

"I think North Korea has typically responded to threats with threats, to provocations with provocations," said Kelsey Davenport, director for nonproliferation policy at the Arms Control Association. "In part, North Korea is responding to the dangerous and bellicose rhetoric of President Trump."

Still, Davenport sees an opening for negotiations, noting that North Korea has said it would not negotiate while under hostile threat. "I read that as keeping the door open for negotiations, if the United States rolls back its more hostile posturing and rhetoric."

2018: An Opening for Talks

As his country prepared to host the Winter Olympics, South Korean President Moon Jae-in reached out to North Korea—inviting athletes from the North to march with their Southern counterparts in the opening ceremony under one flag. Kim Jong-un accepted the invitation and sent his sister as a representative. The détente offered an opening, and a senior North Korean official who attended the closing ceremony indicated that the North was willing to talk with the United States.

In early March, news broke that Kim Jong-un had invited President Trump to meet for negotiations about North Korea's nuclear program. The White House said President Trump had accepted the invitation, and he tweeted that the North Korean leader spoke to South Korean representatives about denuclearization, not just a freeze. He continued [in his tweet], "Great progress being made but sanctions will remain until an agreement is reached. Meeting being planned!"

In mid-April, Trump confirmed reports that CIA Director Mike Pompeo made a top-secret trip to meet Kim Jong-un in North Korea in late March, the highest-level contact since [then-U.S. Secretary of State Madeleine] Albright visited in 2000. The meeting came shortly after Pompeo was nominated for [the position of] secretary of state.

On April 20, North Korea announced that it would suspend nuclear and missile testing, and shut down the site where its six previous nuclear tests were carried out.

In early May, Trump announced a date and location for the anticipated summit: Singapore, on June 12th. Less than a week later, the plan was thrown into question when North Korea issued an angry rebuke to remarks by Trump's new national security adviser, John Bolton. Bolton had suggested the U.S. plan to denuclearize North Korea might follow the "Libya model." (In 2003, Libyan leader Muammar Qaddafi gave up his nascent nuclear program in exchange for sanctions relief. He was brutally killed a few years later by U.S.-backed rebels.) After Bolton's statements, North Korea said it would have to "reconsider" its participation in the summit.

Vice President Mike Pence weighed in on May 21, saying in a televised interview: "This will only end like the Libyan model ended if Kim Jong-un doesn't make a deal." North Korea responded a few days later with a furious statement from Vice Foreign Minister Choe Son-hui, calling Pence's remarks "unbridled and impudent." She once again cast doubt on North Korea's participation in the summit if the United States "clings to unlawful and outrageous acts."

On May 24, President Trump cancelled the summit, citing [to Kim Jong-un] the "tremendous anger and open hostility displayed in your most recent statement." But he seemed to leave the door open to future dialogue, thanking North Korea for releasing American hostages and writing, "If you change your mind having to do with this important summit, please do not hesitate to call me or write."

After a White House visit from Kim Jong-un's top deputy and former spymaster Kim Yong-chol on June 1, Trump said the summit was back on.

The unprecedented meeting between a sitting U.S. president and a North Korean leader took place on June 12 in Singapore.

President Trump and Kim Jong-un shook hands, and the statement they signed said Trump "committed to provide security guarantees" to North Korea, and Kim "reaffirmed his firm and unwavering commitment to complete denuclearization of the Korean Peninsula." The statement was short on specifics, but said more negotiations between North Korean officials and Secretary of State Mike Pompeo would be held "at the earliest possible date."

"We had a historic meeting and decided to leave the past behind," Kim told reporters while sitting next to Trump.

"We're very proud of what took place today," Trump said, after both men signed the statement. "I think our whole relationship with North Korea and the Korean Peninsula is going to be a very much different situation than it has in the past."

Media reports noted that the language about disarmament in the statement was similar to agreements in 1994 and 2005 that eventually faltered.

Trump also made what appeared to be a major concession to North Korea, suspending joint military exercises with South Korea, saying the exercises were expensive and "very provocative."

THIS POST WAS MOST RECENTLY UPDATED ON JUNE 12, 2018. IT WAS ORIGINALLY PUBLISHED ON OCTOBER 4, 2017.
USED WITH PERMISSION FROM PBS FRONTLINE

Supporting Question 3

Source C. Text of a speech made by Kim Jong-un on September 22, 2017 in response to the speech made by Donald Trump to the UN General Assembly on September 19, 2017.

https://www.ncnk.org/resources/publications/kju_statement_to_trump.pdf/file_view

According to the National Committee on North Korea (http://www.ncnk.org), the following is the text "of a statement attributed to North Korean leader Kim Jong-un, responding in direct terms to President Donald Trump's remarks about North Korea at the UN General Assembly, in which Trump referred to Kim as 'Rocket Man' and said that if the United States 'is forced to defend itself or its allies, we will have no choice but to totally destroy North Korea.'" Teachers may want students to also read Trump's UN speech, which is accessible at https://www.whitehouse.gov/briefings-statements/remarks-president-trump-72nd-session-united-nations-general-assembly/.

STATEMENT OF THE CHAIRMAN OF THE STATE AFFAIRS COMMISSION OF THE DEMOCRATIC PEOPLE'S REPUBLIC OF KOREA

Pyongyang, September 22 (KCNA)—Respected Supreme Leader Kim Jong Un, chairman of the State Affairs Commission of the DPRK, released a statement on Thursday.

The full text of the statement reads:

The speech made by the U.S. president in his maiden address on the UN arena in the prevailing serious circumstances, in which the situation on the Korean peninsula has been rendered tense as never before and is inching closer to a touch-and-go state, is arousing worldwide concern.

Shaping the general idea of what he would say, I expected he would make stereotyped, prepared remarks a little different from what he used to utter in his office on the spur of the moment as he had to speak on the world's biggest official diplomatic stage.

But, far from making remarks of any persuasive power that can be viewed to be helpful to defusing tension, he made unprecedented rude nonsense one has never heard from any of his predecessors.

A frightened dog barks louder.

I'd like to advise Trump to exercise prudence in selecting words and to be considerate of whom he speaks to when making a speech in front of the world.

The mentally deranged behavior of the U.S. president openly expressing on the UN arena the unethical will to "totally destroy" a sovereign state, beyond the boundary of threats of regime change or overturn of social system, makes even those with normal thinking faculty think about discretion and composure.

His remarks remind me of such words as "political layman" and "political heretic" which were in vogue in reference to Trump during his presidential election campaign.

After taking office Trump has rendered the world restless through threats and blackmail against all countries in the world. He is unfit to hold the prerogative of supreme command of a country, and he is surely a rogue and a gangster fond of playing with fire, rather than a politician.

His remarks which described the U.S. option through straightforward expression of his will have convinced me, rather than frightening or stopping me, that the path I chose is correct and that it is the one I have to follow to the last.

Now that Trump has denied the existence of and insulted me and my country in front of the eyes of the world and made the most ferocious declaration of a war in history that he would destroy the DPRK, we will consider with seriousness exercising of a corresponding, highest level of hard-line countermeasure in history.

Action is the best option in treating the dotard who, hard of hearing, is uttering only what he wants to say.

As a man representing the DPRK and on behalf of the dignity and honor of my state and people and on my own, I will make the man holding the prerogative of the supreme command in the U.S. pay dearly for his speech calling for totally destroying the DPRK.

This is not a rhetorical expression loved by Trump.

I am now thinking hard about what response he could have expected when he allowed such eccentric words to trip off his tongue.

Whatever Trump might have expected, he will face results beyond his expectation. I will surely and definitely tame the mentally deranged U.S. dotard with fire.